All that is beautiful God has made.
He sets eternity in our hearts.
No one can fathom the work of God
Where it will end, or where it starts.

—Ecclesiastes 3:11

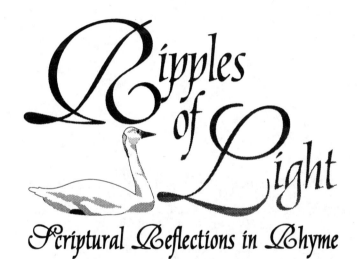

Ripples of Light

of

Light

Scriptural Reflections in Rhyme

Copyright Bernard Williams
Bible Editor, James C. Hefley, B.A., M.Div., Litt.D., Ph.D.
Poetry Editor, Mary Leah Christmas
Copy Editors, Marti Hefley, Steve Grubbs, Cyndi Allison, Brittany McFarland
Design Editor, Cyndi Allison
Cover Photo, Andy Allison
Cover Design, Cyndi Allison
Printed in the United States of America by Dickinson Press
Library of Congress Number 94-077459
ISBN 0-929292-78-2

John 1:1-10

1 *In the beginning was the Word,*
The Word was God also.
The Word was also with God from
2 *The beginning quite long ago.*

3 *Through Him all things were made, apart*
From Him naught was created.
And through the Word all things have
come,
As God Himself has stated.

4 *In Him was, and in Him is life,*
The very Light of men.
5 *The Light shines in darkness; the*
Darkness does not comprehend.

6 *A man named John was sent from God,*
7 *As a witness to the light,*
That all men might believe in Him
And do the things that are right.

8 *Though John himself was not the*
Light,
A witness to it he'd be.
9 *The light would open each man's eyes,*
So he might truly see.

10 *He was in the world when it was made;*
The world was made through Him;
But by the world He was not known:
Their eyes were very dim. ✝

Genesis 1:1-5, 25 & 26

1 *In the beginning God created*
The heavens and the earth,
Everything we see today
By our God, was given birth.

2 *The earth was void and without form,*
There were no plants or trees;
Darkness o'er the surface reigned,
And spread across the seas.

The Spirit of God moved,
Across the waters' face.
3 *God said, "Let light be there,"*
And light filled all the space.

4 *God saw the light, and it was good:*
For all things God does right,
5 *He divided light from darkness*
And thus made day and night.

The evening and the morning were
The first day of creation;
God's mighty power was displayed
In every situation.

25 *Day by day our God created*
Land, herbs, and heavenly light,
Fish, fowl, beasts, and cattle
Each was a wonderful sight.

26 *Then God said, "Let us make man,*
In Our own image he shall be,
Yes, after Our own likeness
Mankind's features all shall see.

"We'll let him have dominion o'er
Birds, fish and livestock too
And take control of creeping things
That move along in view." ✝

Psalm 1

1 *How blessed is the man who with*
The wicked does not walk,
Or in the paths of sinners stand,
Nor with the scoffers mock.

2 *But in the law of the Lord*
He truly finds delight,
In God's law he meditates,
Throughout the day and night.

3 *He will be like a spreading tree*
Planted beside a stream
Which yields much fruit in season, and
Thus fulfills his dream.

Its leaf does not wither, and
He prospers in all he tries;

God pours His blessings out on him,
And dries tears from his eyes.

4 *With the wicked it is not this way;*
Like chaff they blow in the wind.
5 *They cannot stand in judgment;*
They will come to an evil end.

In the assembly of the righteous
No sinner will be found.
6 *For the Lord knows the righteous,*
But the wicked shall not rebound.

The Lord watches and He sees
The path the righteous cherish,
While the ungodly go their way,
The wicked shall surely perish. ✝

Genesis 3:1-7

1 *Now the serpent was more subtle,*
Than any beast of the field
Made by the Lord of creation,
To the woman he appealed.

He asked, "Did God really say to you
Of no tree you shall eat
In the beautiful garden he created
With good fruit so sweet?"

2 *The woman replied unto the serpent,*
"We may eat of any tree
3 *Except of the tree of knowledge,*
God said, 'That's not for thee.'

"He said we are not to eat of it,
Though it's pleasant to the eye;
For the day we touch the fruit
Is the day that we will die."

4 *Then the serpent said to the woman,*
"You surely shall not die,
5 *God knows if you eat this fruit,*
It will open up your eye.

"Then you will become like God
Knowing evil from what's right."
6 *And as the woman looked at the tree*
It seemed pleasant to her sight.

The fruit looked so good and sweet,
She thought, "What Satan said is true."
She ate, then said to Adam,
"Eat and be wise too."

7 *Then their eyes were fully opened,*
They knew that they were bare;
They quickly sewed fig leaves together
To have something they could wear. ✞

Psalm 2:1-12

1 *Why do all the nations conspire*
And plot together as one?
2 *Kings throng to stand against the Lord,*
Against His Anointed One.

3 *"Let us break their bonds," they all say,*
As they rant and rave and fuss,
"Let's toss their fetters far away,
And cast off their cords from us."

4 *God enthroned in heaven shall laugh;*
He will scoff at their vain pride.
5 *He will speak to them in anger;*
And they'll all be terrified.

6 *Upon the holy hill of Zion*
I have installed my king,
7 *I will declare to everyone,*
The Lord's decree I'll bring.

"You're my Son, today I become
Your Father," He said to me.
8 *"Ask of Me, and I will give*
Your birthright by My decree.

"Yes, I will make all the nations,
Your inheritance, and more,
The ends of the earth are yours, and
The things it holds in store.

9 *"You'll rule them with an iron rod;*
They'll shatter like earthen-ware."
10 *So therefore, kings, do be wise*
You've been warned, so now take care.

11 *Serve the Lord with fear and trembling,*
With trembling you should rejoice.
12 *Kiss the Son, and beware His wrath,*
His refuge should be your choice. ✝

Galatians 3:11-29

11 *Before God it is evident,*
By law none is justified.
"The righteous man shall live by faith,"
Under the law he cannot hide.

12 *For the law is not of faith,*
It can only condemn.
"But he who tries to do these things,
The same shall live by them."

13 *Christ redeemed us from the law's curse,*
Became a curse for you and me.
For it is written: "Cursed is one
Who hangs upon a tree."

14 *He redeemed us so Abraham's*
Blessing might come to the Gentile,
Through Christ, so by faith they'd receive
The Spirit and be reconciled.

That we might have the promise of
The Spirit of our Lord;
Through the faith that we have in Him,
Salvation is our reward.

15 *Brethren I speak in human terms;*
Even a man's contract
When it's ratified, no one
Shall add or take it back.

16 *Promises were said to Abraham*
And to his seed alone.
He wasn't referring to many seeds,
This I would have made known.

He did not say, "And to your seeds,"
He spoke of only one,
"And this one Seed is Jesus Christ,
God's blessed only Son."

10

17 *What I say to you is: The law*
Which God gave to our nation,
Came years after Abraham, it
Wasn't a prior creation.

It doesn't nullify God's promise,
Not even if it tried.
You cannot void a covenant
Which God has ratified.

18 *If our birthright is built on law,*
It's not on promise based;
But God promised it to Abraham;
It cannot be erased.

19 *Why then did God give us the law?*
It was given because of sin,
having been ordained by angels
By a mediator for men.

To stay until the Seed should come
To whom the promise was made,
Then when the Seed should then appear,
The law away should fade.

20 *A mediator isn't just for one,*
But God is one, you see.
21 *Is law contrary to God's promise?*
No, this could never be.

If a law had been given which
Could impart life to thee
Then Christ need not have died, for the
Law would have set us free.

Then righteousness indeed would then
Upon the law be based,
And if we didn't keep it, we'd
Before God be disgraced.

22 The Scripture put men under sin;
But those who in faith believe
In Jesus Christ our holy Lord
The promise they will receive.

23 But before faith came to us, we
Were in law's custody
Being shut up in faith which is
Revealed to you and me.

24 Therefore, the law becomes our tutor,
To Christ the law would lead,
That we'd be justified by faith
If His word's we'd only heed.

25 But now that faith has come, we no
Longer need one to teach
26 For we are sons of God through faith
In Jesus whom we preach.

27 For all are baptized into Christ
Are clothed in Christ, you see,
28 There's no difference 'tween Jew or Greek
Or between slave or free.

There is neither male nor female,
29 For in Christ you are one,
Through promise, heirs of Abraham
By faith in God's own Son. ✞

Psalm 28

1 *Oh, Lord, my Rock, I cry to You,*
Without You I have no breath.
If You are silent, I'll be like
Those in the pit of death.

2 *Hear my supplications, Lord,*
When I lift my tearful face,
When I lift my hands up to You,
Toward Your most Holy Place.

3 *Don't count me with the wicked,*
Or with the workers of iniquity,
Those speaking peace to neighbors,
While planning an evil deed.

4 *Repay them as they've paid others,*
According to their wickedness,
According to the works that they do,
Repay them with distress.

5 *For they disregard the works of God,*
With what He's done with His hands;
He'll break them down, not build them up,
For they ignore His commands.

6 *But I say, "Blessed be the Lord,*
Because He has heard my voice;
He listened to my supplication,
Now in Him I will rejoice."

7 *The Lord is my strength and shield,*
I trust in Him alone,
He helps me and I do exult,
And praise Him with glad song.

8 *The Lord God is His people's strength,*
A refuge for His anointed;
9 *Defend Your people, bless the chosen,*
Feed, lift up Your appointed. ✟

Genesis 9:1, 8-16

1 *God blessed Noah and his sons, said,*
"Be fruitful and multiply,
By you I will replenish the earth
And I'll always be nearby."

8 *Then God spoke to Noah again,*
He spoke to his sons too,
9 *"I'll make with you My covenant,*
And with your seed follow through.

10 *"It will be with every living creature,*
With birds, cattle and beasts;
All that go from the ark, now
That the great flood has ceased.

11 *"I'll make with you My covenant,*
I'll not cut off all men,
Neither shall there be a flood
That will destroy the earth again.

12 *"This is the token I will give,*
Signifying My pledge to you,
It includes all living creatures
And all their descendants too.

13 *"I'll set My bow in the clouds,*
And My token it will be,
For the covenant which I do make
Between the earth and you and Me.

14 *"And it shall come to pass that when*
O'er the earth I send a cloud,
A rainbow will be seen, and then,
15 *I'll remember what I vowed.*

"That the waters won't become a flood
Destroying flesh of every kind;
16 *The rainbow shall be in the cloud,*
A token of what I have in mind." ✝

Psalm 4

1 *Hear me, Lord, when I call,*
O God of my righteousness!
Be gracious and hear my prayer;
Relieve me from distress.

2 *Oh sons of men, how long will my*
Glory be a reproach to you?
How long will you love worthless things
And seek after falsehood too?

3 *Know that the Lord has set apart*
The godly man for Himself;
The Lord hears me when I call;
Puts not my prayers on a shelf.

4 *Tremble and commit no sin;*
Meditate upon your bed;
5 *Be still and offer sacrifice;*
Trust Him, the living bread.

6 *Many ask, "Who will show us good?"*
My Lord, lift up the light
Of your countenance on us;
Help us do what is right.

7 *You've put more gladness in my heart*
Than when grain and wine abound.
8 *I will lie down and sleep,*
In Your arms I'm safe and sound. ✝

Acts 2:1-41

1 On the day of Pentecost,
All were gathered in one place,
2 When a noise like violent wind
From heaven suddenly raced.

It filled all the house where they were;
3 Fire rested on each head,
4 The Holy Spirit filled them all
And by Him all were led.

They began speaking in other tongues,
As the Spirit had them say.
5 Devout Jews from every nation
Were in Jerusalem that day.

6 When the crowd heard the noise, they
Came together at that place,
All were amazed, for each heard
The language of their own race.

7 The crowd, quite startled, said, "These are
Galileans, we'd have sworn,
8 How is it now we hear them in
The tongue to which we were born?"

9 Parthians, Medes, and Elamites,
Mesopotamian dwellers too;
From Judea, Pontus, Cappadocia;
And also from Asia came the Jews.

10 Phyrgia and Pamphylia,
From Egypt and Cyrene where,
These visitors came from Rome,
Both Jews and proselytes were there.

11 Cretans and Arabians awed,
They listened without debate,
For they heard in their own tongue
Of God and His wonders great.

12 They all remained mystified at
This great and amazing sign.
Some asked, "What do you think it means?"
13 Some answered, "They're full of wine."

14 Peter stood with the eleven and said,
Raising his voice to be heard,
"Men of Judea and Jerusalem,
Listen, give heed to my word.

15 "These men aren't drunk as you suppose
At just the third hour of the day;
16 The prophet Joel spoke of this,
Listen to what he had to say:

17 "God says, 'Now when the last days come
My Spirit I'll pour on all;
Sons and daughters will prophesy,
In visions, young men I'll call.

" 'And your old men shall dream dreams,
And bond slaves will stand and cry,
18 On them too shall My Spirit fall;
They'll also prophesy.

19 " 'I will show wonders in the sky,
And signs on the earth below.
Blood, fire and vapors of smoke,
These signs I want you to know.

20 " 'The moon shall be turned to blood,
And the sun shall become dark,
Before the Lord's day will arrive
When all will see His mark.

21 " 'Many will be greatly concerned;
On God's mercy they will call,
And all who call upon the Lord,
Shall be saved, one and all.'

22 "Men of Israel, hear these words;
Jesus Christ, the Nazarene,
A man approved by God to you
Through the miracles you've seen.

"Miracles God performed through Him,
And the wonders God did show,
But I needn't speak to you of this;
For this you already know.

23 "Christ was delivered up according
To a predetermined plan,
God in advance knew all of this;
He was nailed to a cross by man.

24 "Although He was put to death
God raised Him up again,
Death's grip could not hold Him and
He was freed from death's pain.

25 "For David said concerning Him,
'My right hand He has taken.
His presence is ever before me,
That I may not be shaken.

26 " 'Therefore, my heart was very glad;
And my tongue exalts His name,
Causing me to abide in hope
For He's always just the same.

27 " 'You will not leave me to hell
Nor let Thy Holy One decay.
28 You've made known the way of life
In Thy presence I'm glad always.'

29 "Now of the patriarch, David,
To you I confidently say,
Both that he died and he was buried,
His tomb is with us today.

30 *"And because he was a prophet*
To him God did make known
That one of his descendants would
One day sit on his throne.

31 *"He spoke of the resurrection,*
And of that glorious day.
Christ would not be left in Hades,
Neither would His flesh decay.

32 *"This Jesus God raised up again,*
We're witnesses of this fact.
The resurrection was not a dream
Nor a great magic act.

33 *"Hence, having been exalted, to*
God's right hand He is near.
He's poured forth God's Holy Spirit,
Which you both see and hear.

34 *"David didn't rise to heaven,*
But he heard God's command,
The Lord said unto my Lord: 'You
Shall sit at My right hand.'

"And the Lord further stated this:
These words He did repeat,
35 *'I shall make your enemies be*
A footstool for your feet.'

36 "Let all the house of Israel know
That although this One died,
God's made Him both Lord and Christ,
Jesus, whom you crucified."

37 Now when they had heard these
        words, their hearts
Were pierced through and through.
Said they to Peter and the apostles,
"Brothers, what'll we do?"

38 And Peter answered all of them,
"Repent now of your sins, I say
And be baptized in Jesus name;
Have your sins forgiven today.

"The Spirit will be given you,
39 For the promise is for all,
Whether they are near or far away,
To all the Lord shall call.

40 "Be saved from this crooked age."
With many words he testified,
And he kept on telling them, "It was
For you that Christ had died."

41 Many believed what Peter preached,
And were baptized in Jesus' name.
All told about three thousand souls
Joined with the fellowship that day. ✝

Genesis 12:1,2 & 17:1-6

1 *Now the Lord had said to Abram,*
"This thing you must do,
Leave your country and your kindred
Go where I'll show you.

2 *"A nation of you I will make,*
My blessing is on you;
I will make your name great,
And you will bless others too."

1 *When Abram was ninety-nine*
The Lord again appeared,
He said, "I am Almighty God,
Walk upright and revere.

2 *"And I will make My covenant,*
Between Me and you,
I'll multiply you exceedingly
In everything you do."

3 *Abram fell on his face,*
God talked with him and said,

4 *"My covenant is made with you,*
By Me you will be led.

"Many nations shall come from you,
From the children which you bear,
Because of the covenant I make with you
You are safe within My care.

5 *"And you shall have a change of name,*
No more will you be Abram,
You'll be the father of many nations,
You'll be called Abraham.

6 *"I will make you very fruitful,*
I'll make nations come from you;
Kings shall come from your seed
I've said it, therefore, it's true." ✞

Exodus 3

1 *Moses kept the flock of his father-in-law,*
A priest and Midianite,
Led the flock to the back of the desert,
To Mount Horeb where he saw a sight.

2 *The angel of the Lord appeared,*
In the midst of a bush on fire;
The bush burned, but wasn't consumed,
To investigate was his desire.

3 *Moses said, "I will turn aside,*
And see this bush which is nigh."
4 *God called his name from the bush,*
Moses replied, "Lord, here am I."

5 *The Lord said, "Come no closer,*
Take your shoes from off your feet;
You are standing on holy ground,
Almighty God, here you'll meet.

6 *"I'm the God of your father, Abraham,*
Isaac and of Jacob too."
Moses hid his face, for he feared God,
He was not sure what he should do.

7 *"I've seen the affliction of My people*
In Egypt, I've heard their cry;
I know their sorrows," said the Lord.
8 *"The time to deliver them is nigh.*

"I'll bring them from Egypt to a land,
Where milk and honey flows;
Where the Canaanite, Hittite, Amorite,
Perizzite, Hivite and Jebusite goes.

9 *"The cry of Israel has come to Me,*
And I've seen how they are oppressed;
10 *So now I'm sending you to Pharaoh,*
To lead them out, so they'll be blessed." ✝

Psalm 23

1 *My shepherd is the Lord*
Who gives me all my needs;
2 *He makes me lie in pastures green,*
By waters still He leads.

3 *My Lord He doth restore my soul;*
On righteous paths He guides.
He does this for His dear name's sake,
While I walk by His side.

4 *Yea, though I walk through the valley*
Where the shadow of death hovers near,
I know that the Lord is with me,
And no evil I need fear.

His rod and staff they comfort me;
5 *A table before me He doth prepare,*
And though my enemies are all about,
I need not fear, He's there!

My head He doth anoint with oil,
With His love my cup runs o'er.
6 *Goodness and mercy shall follow me,*
I'll dwell in His house evermore. ✝

Job 1:1-12

1 There was a man whose name was Job
He lived in Uz with his family,
He feared God and avoided evil,
He was upright, as he ought to be.

2 Seven sons were born to Job,
And he had three daughters, too;
3 He was the richest man of the East,
As all around him knew.

He owned seven thousand sheep,
Three thousand camels his estate bore,
Five hundred yoke of oxen,
Of female donkeys, twenty five score.

4 His sons feasted in their houses,
Each day one son served as host;
Their sisters there did join them,
And with them ate and drank a toast.

5 When their feasting days were over,
His children, Job would sanctify;
Early in the morning he would rise,
And unto God he would cry.

He'd offer burnt sacrifices for each,
Saying, "Perhaps they have sinned.
They may have cursed God in their hearts."
Their relations with God, he would mend.

6 There was a day when the angels of God
To the Lord themselves presented,
And Satan also came among them,
Although of evil he had not repented.

7 And the Lord spoke to Satan there:
"Where are you coming from?"
"From going to and fro on the
Earth, today I have come."

8 The Lord said, "Have you noticed Job,
There's none like him on earth?
He's a perfect and upright man,
And full of joy and mirth.

"He fears God and despises evil,
Always seeks to do what's right,
He always serves and honors Me,
He is precious in my sight."

9 "Does Job fear God for naught?"
    asked Satan.
10 "You've made a hedge on every side,
You've blessed the works of his hands,
Increasing his wealth in all he's tried.

11 "Put forth your hand and take all
    he has,
Then he will curse you to Your face,
He will blame you for the loss of his wealth,
And will consider his life a disgrace."

12 Then the Lord unto Satan said,
"All Job has I place in your hand,
But you must not touch Job himself,
These conditions you understand."

Satan went forth from the Lord's presence,
Thinking, "Job will soon be mine,
I'll bring trouble a plenty on him,
I'll test him time after time." ✝

25

Job 42:1-8, 10

1 Then Job answered the Lord and said,
"I know there's nothing You cannot do,
2 No purpose of Yours can be held back,
Wisdom and power lies with You.

3 "I've said things without knowing,
I spoke of what I did not understand;
Things too fine for me ever to know,
I've received from your gracious hand.

4 "You said, 'Listen, and I will speak,
I'll ask and you must answer Me.'
5 I have heard You with my ears,
But now, You, Lord, my eyes do see.

"I know You are the Almighty,
And I know Your ways are just;
6 Wherefore, I now abhor myself,
And repent in ashes and dust."

7 After the Lord had spoken to Job,
He addressed Eliphas, the Temanite.
"I'm angry against you and your friends;
You've not spoken to Me what is right.

8 "Therefore make a sacrifice.
Take seven bulls and seven rams, too.
Then you go up to my servant, Job,
And he will pray for you.

"For Job's sake I will accept you,
And your folly I will forgive,
You didn't speak of me, as he did,
But for his prayer, I'll let you live."

10 When Job knelt and prayed for his friends
His trials and troubles were o'er.
God restored his former state,
Giving him twice what he had before. ✞

Romans 3:20 - 26

20 By works of the law none are
Justified in God's sight;
For it's through the law we're taught
To know sin and what's right.

21 But now apart from the law, God's
Righteousness is manifested;
To which the law and the prophets
All witnessed and attested.

22 God's righteousness comes through faith
In Jesus to those who believe;
No difference between Jew or Greek;
His grace they will all receive.

23 For all men have committed sin,
Of God's glory they've fallen short.
Unworthy they are of heaven,
According to God's report.

24 Justification is given as
A free gift of God's grace
Because of the ransom, Christ did pay,
We can stand before His face.

25 He was given to us by God
As atonement for our sin;
He gave His blood to save us, and
Through faith, we enter in.

He gave His blood to demonstrate
Righteousness that will last;
God in His forbearance, looked
Over sins done in the past.

26 He proves His righteousness,
The Just and the Justifier,
Through faith in Jesus, all can
Escape God's judgment dire. ✟

1 John 1:1 - 2:1-5

1 *That which was from the beginning,*
Those things which we have heard,
Have seen with our own eyes about
Jesus Christ, the Word,

Which we held with our own hands
Concerning the word of life,
2 *The life was manifested here*
In this, our world of strife.

We've seen Him, bear witness and proclaim
The eternal life to you.
This one was with the Father and
Manifested to us, too.

3 *And all that we have seen and heard*
To you we now proclaim
That you may join the fellowship
As Christ's Lordship you claim.

Together with the Father, and
With His Son, Christ, we meet,
4 *And these things we write unto you*
That your joy may be complete.

5 *From Him we heard this message and*
We announce it unto you
That you may also believe in Him
And know our words are true.

Our God is light itself, in Him
No darkness can be found.
6 *If we say we walk with Him, but*
In darkness we are bound,

Then we do not practice truth,
In fact we live a lie.
7 *But if we do walk in the light*
Then our Lord is nearby.

For Christ Himself is the light, in
The fellowship of men,
It is the blood of Jesus Christ
That cleanses us from sin.

8 If we say we have no sin then
Ourselves we do deceive,
And the truth is not in us and
Our Lord we can't receive.

9 If we our sins then confess, He
Is faithful to forgive
And cleanse us from unrighteousness
If for Him we will live.

10 If we say that we have not sinned
Then we make Him a liar,
And His word is not in us, which
Bring consequences dire.

2:1 My children I write to you that
You not fall into sin,
But if you do, our advocate
Will make you right again.

Our helper, Jesus Christ the righteous,
2 Is the propitiation
For our sins, and not ours alone,
But for those of every nation.

3 We may be sure we know Him if
We do as he demands,
4 The one who says I know Him, but
Does not keep his commands

Is both a liar and a deceiver,
The truth's in him not found;
5 But whoever keeps His word, in
Them God's Word doth abound. ✟

Exodus 20:1-24

1 *The Lord spoke and said these words:*
2 *"I am the Lord, the God of Israel.*
I brought you out of Egyptian bondage,
With greater power than man can tell.

3 *"No other gods shall you have before Me.*
4 *No graven image shall you make;*
Of any likeness in heaven, earth, or water
For false worship shall you take.

5 *"You shall not bow down or serve them,*
For a jealous God I be;
On the children I place judgment
For the fathers who hate Me.

6 *"But I show mercy unto thousands,*
Those who love and keep My commands
7 *You shall not take God's name in vain,*
You will not guiltless before me stand.

8 *"Remember the sabbath and keep it holy,*
9 *Six days shall your work be done,*
10 *On the seventh is the sabbath,*
The day of rest for everyone.

It's the sabbath of the Lord your God,
Thou shall do no work that day,
No, not any in your household,
Or those who with you stay.

11 *"In six days the Lord made heaven*
The earth, the sea and all therein,
He rested and blessed the sabbath,
To be kept holy by all men.

12 *"Honor your father and mother, so*
Your days may be long in the land;
The land which is a gift from God,
And where you follow God's command.

13 *"You shall not kill your fellow man,*
14 *Nor shall you commit adultery,*
15 *You shall not steal from anyone,*
16 *Nor shall false witness come from thee.*

17 *"You shall not covet your neighbor's house,*
Nor shall you covet your neighbor's wife;
Nor his maidservant or his ox,
Covetousness will lead to strife."

18 *When they saw thunder and lightning,*
And they heard the trumpet sound;
When they saw smoke on the mountain,
The people trembled all around.

They retreated to a distance,
Where they gazed with continued fear
19 *Said, "Moses, speak and we will listen;*
If God speaks, we'll die here."

20 *Moses spoke unto the people,*
"You don't need to be afraid,
For our God has come to test you,
So from sin you will be stayed."

21 *Then the people stood afar off,*
While in darkness Moses drew near
To the thick cloud where God spoke,
While the people remained in fear.

22 *There the Lord said to Moses,*
"Tell the Israelites what I've done.
I have spoken to you from Heaven,
I am God, the Holy One.

23 *"You shall not make gods of silver,*
Nor shall you make gods of gold.
24 *Make for me an earthen altar,*
I will come and bless your soul." ✝

Psalm 44:1-8

1 *We have heard with our ears, O God,*
Our fathers have told the tale,
Of what You did in days long past
They have told us without fail.

2 *Your hand drove the heathen out, then*
Put our fathers in the land,
You made our fathers flourish, and
Crushed the pagans with Your hand.

3 *Our fathers did not win the land*
It was won not with their sword,
Nor were saved by their strong arm,
It was all by Your accord.

The victory was by Your hand,
Came by Your arm from above.

It was by the light of Your face,
For our fathers You did love.

4 *You are my King, You are my God,*
You saved Jacob from his woes.
5 *Through Your name we push back enemies,*
We trample all our foes.

6 *I will not trust in my bow, nor*
My sword for my victories.
7 *You put our rivals to shame, and*
Saved us from our enemies.

8 *We'll forever brag on our God,*
Your holy name we will praise,
And we will continue to boast
Yes, forever and always. ♱

Acts 4:7-13

7 They placed them in the center, and
Questions they began to ask,
"By what name or what power have
You accomplished this task?"

8 Filled with the Spirit, Peter said,
"Rulers and elders of the Jews,
9 If we're on trial for what we've done,
Let us bring you this good news.

10 "You want to know how this lame man
Stands here before you well.
Let it be known to all of you
And all of Israel;

"By Jesus Christ the Nazarene
Condemned and crucified
Whom God raised from the dead, and is
Today by God's right side.

"By His name was this man made well,
In this His mighty power's shown.
11 The stone rejected by the builders,
Has become the cornerstone.

12 "Salvation is in no one else;
There is no other name
By which we find our salvation,
For this is why He came."

13 When the rulers and elders heard
Peter and John speaking so,
They were astonished and amazed,
Sensing how little they did know.

These were two ordinary men
Whose words rang with authority.
They marvelled and took note they'd been
With Jesus, in His ministry. ✝

Joshua 1:1-3; 5-9

1 *It came to pass after Moses died,*
The Lord spoke to Joshua, son of Nun:
Joshua had been Moses' lieutenant,
And had witnessed what God had done.

2 *The Lord said, "Moses, My servant is dead.*
Now cross the Jordan River,
Lead the people into the land beyond
Which to them I will deliver.

3 *"Wherever the soul of your foot treads,*
That is the land I have given to you;
This is the promise I made to Moses,
And to you this promise I renew.

5 *"No one can stand before you there;*
As I was with Moses, so I'll be with you;
I will not fail you, nor will I forget,
I'll be with you in all that you do.

6 *"Be of good courage and be strong,*
Among this people you'll divide the land.
I promised your fathers it as an inheritance,
Now you'll receive it by My hand.

7 *"Be you strong and very courageous,*
Keep all the law that Moses gave you;
From it, turn not to the right or the left,
That you may prosper in all you do.

8 *"This law shall not depart from your mouth.*
Meditate on it day and night.
Observe all that is written therein,
And in you I will find delight.

"Prosperous you will make your way,
And success will surely come to you.
9 *Be strong, courageous and fear not;*
I will be with you in all you do." ✝

Psalm 103:1-13, 17

1 *Bless the Lord, oh my soul,*
And all that is within me,
Bless the Lord's holy name,
2 *Forget not His benefits I see.*

3 *He forgives you all your sins,*
And He heals your every infirmity,
4 *He redeems your life from destruction,*
With kindness and mercy He loves thee.

5 *He satisfies thy mouth with sweet things,*
As the eagle thy youth He doth renew;
6 *Righteousness and judgment for thee,*
The Lord gives the oppressed their just due.

7 *His will He made known unto Moses,*
And to the children of Israel His ways;
8 *The Lord is gracious and merciful,*
Slow to anger and merciful all the days.

9 *He will not always chide His people,*
He'll not always be angry with men,
10 *Nor reward us according to our iniquities;*
He has not dealt with us after our sin.

11 *For as the heaven is high above the earth,*
His mercy is great to those who fear Him.
12 *As far as the east is from the west,*
He removes their transgressions from them.

13 *As a father is compassionate to his child,*
He pities those who in Him place their trust,
For he knows how our bodies were fashioned,
And remembers how they turn to dust.

17 *But for all of those who fear Him,*
His mercy will go on forever and ever;
He will bless His children's children,
And help them in all they endeavor. ✝

1 Corinthians 13

1 *If I speak like men or angels,*
But no love in me is found,
I am but a clanging cymbal,
Or brass that so loudly sounds.

2 *If I've the gift of prophecy*
And all mysteries understand
And if I have the faith needed
To move mountains in the land;

3 *It's nothing if I have not love;*
It will not help anymore
If I give everything I have
To feed all the wretched poor.

And if I should give my body
To be burned for the Lord's sake,
But do not have love, it's nothing,
No gain or credit can I take.

4 *Love's patient; love is kind; in love*
Jealousy does not abide.
Love does not brag about itself;
It's not filled with foolish pride.

5 *Love is not rude or self-seeking*
In anger love does not flame.
Love does not count wrongs suffered,
Nor does it keep record of blame.

6 *Love does not exult in evil*
Love finds in evil no delight.
But love rejoices in the truth,
Love always basks in truth's light.

7 *Love bears all things, believes all things;*
In all things love finds hope.
Love endures all and will not fail,
For with all things love can cope.

8 *If there are gifts of prophecy,*
They will all vanish some day.
And if there are tongues, they shall cease
Even knowledge will pass away.

9 *For our knowledge is imperfect,*
We just prophesy in part.
10 *But when the good and perfect comes,*
The incomplete will depart.

11 *When I was but a little child,*
I thought and talked childishly.
When I became a man I then
Put childish things behind me.

12 *Now we see in a mirror dim,*
But then God's face we'll be shown;
Now I know in part, but someday,
I'll know as I have been known.

13 *And now this is all that remains,*
Faith, hope and love, and you'll see
That while all these are important,
Love is greatest of the three. ☩

Acts 16:25-34

25 *At midnight Paul and Silas prayed.*
And with hymns God they praised.
The other prisoners could hear them
As they their voices raised.

26 *Then suddenly a great earthquake came,*
And the prison house did shake.
Their chains were loosed, the doors flew open,
27 *The jailor came wide awake.*

Seeing the prison doors were open
His sharp sword he drew out.
For he believed the prisoners had
Escaped, without a doubt.

He was about to kill himself, when
28 *Paul cried, "Do yourself no harm!*
For we are all here in the prison,
You have no cause for alarm."

29 *The jailor called for lights, and then*
He quickly rushed inside.
He fell at Paul and Silas' feet,
His fear he could not hide.

30 *He brought them out and asked, "How can*
This salvation now come to me?"
31 *They said, "Believe and Jesus Christ*
Will save you and your family."

32 *They spoke God's message to him, and*
To all who gathered there.
33 *He washed their wounds that very hour,*
As in God's love he shared.

He was baptized without delay,
His household was baptized too.
34 *He set food before them in his house,*
Rejoicing in what God could do. ☧

Psalm 91:1-11

1 *He that dwells in the secret place*
Of the Most High, shall abide
'Neath the shadow of the Almighty,
Who is always by his side.

2 *Of the dear Lord, I will say,*
He is my refuge, my fortress too;
My God in whom I'll always trust
In everything I say and do.

3 *From the pestilence He will save you,*
And deliver from the fowler's snare,
4 *He will cover you with His feathers,*
'Neath His wings you'll trust His care.

His truth shall be your shield and buckler,
5 *You'll not fear terrors at night,*
Nor in the day will you be afraid
When arrows take their flight.

6 *Do not fear the pestilence*
Coming down the dark pathway,
Nor the plague that wastes many lives
At the hour of noon each day.

7 *A thousand shall fall at your side,*
Ten thousand at your right hand,
But the plague will not come near to you,
For beside you God will stand.

8 *The wicked are rewarded for evil deeds,*
Which you will only see with your eye,
9 *Since you've made your refuge the Lord,*
You will live with the Most High.

10 *He shall let no evil befall you here,*
Nor plagues come near where you dwell.
11 *His angels shall have charge over you;*
Evil around you they will quell. ✞

Hebrews 8

1 *The point is that we have a high priest*
Who sits at God's right hand,
Sits on the throne of majesty,
In the heavens, oh so grand,

2 *A minister in the sacred tent,*
A sanctuary not man made,
But one pitched by God Himself and
Its glory will not fade.

3 *For every high priest is appointed*
To offer sacrifices and gifts,
But this high priest must have something
To offer to uplift.

4 *Now if He were on earth, He would*
Not be a priest at all,
Since there are priests who give according
To the Mosaic law.

5 *Those priests serve a copy and shadow*
Of the heavenly thing,
Just as Moses was warned by God,
Instructed by God, saying,

"See that you make the sacred tent
According to My plan,"
For it was shown him on the mountain,
A pattern not from man.

6 *But now Christ has a ministry*
Much better than the old,
The one He mediates is better
Since better promises it holds.

7 *For if that first covenant had been*
Faultless and kept by men
A second would not have been needed
To save men from their sin.

8 *He finds fault with them, saying, "A*
New covenant I will make
With Israel and with Judah,
I do it for their sake,

9 *"Not like the covenant I made*
With their fathers in a distant land;
To lead them out of Egypt, then,
I took them by the hand.

"They did not keep My covenant,
They found it hard to bear;
Therefore, I said unto them all,
'For you I will not care.'

10 *"This new pact that I will make*
With the house of Israel.

After those days," says the Lord,
"Within them I will dwell.

11 *"They'll not teach everyone his fellow;*
'Know the Lord,' They will not say,
For everyone will know the Lord,
The least and the greatest, they.

12 *"For I will be merciful, all their*
Iniquities I'll forgive;
Their sins I'll remember no more, for
In Me they truly live."

13 *When He said, "A new covenant,"*
The first became obsolete.
Thus, old and worthless, it would vanish,
Its terms He would delete. ✞

Leviticus 26:1-12

1 "Make no idol or graven image,
A standing image you shall not rear,
In all of your land, in no place
Shall an idol image of stone appear.

"For I am the Lord your God,
Before an image you shall not bow.
2 Keep My sabbaths, honor my presence,
To the Lord God, keep your vow.

3 "Walk in My laws, keep My commands,
4 And I'll send rain for your fields;
The trees will produce much fruit, and
The land will give you bumper yields.

5 "Threshings shall last while grapes ripen,
Gathering grapes when time comes to sow;
All the year you'll have food abundant,
All the year you will safely go.

6 "Peace I will give you where you live,
You can lie down and not be afraid;
I'll chase evil beasts from your crops,
And no army your fields will raid.

7 "You will run enemies out of your land.
They will be driven from your sight.
8 Five of you shall chase a hundred,
A hundred will put ten thousand to flight.

9 "I'll care for you and make you fruitful;
I will establish My covenant with you;
10 Abundant food will fill your storehouses,
You'll dump the old to make room for new.

11 "I'll set My dwelling in your midst,
You are My people which I won't abhor.
12 I'll walk among you and be your God;
You'll be my people forever more." ✝

Psalm 51:1-12

1 *Oh God, please have mercy on me,*
And give heed to my confession,
In loving kindness and tender mercies,
Please blot out my transgression.

2 *Wash me of my iniquity,*
And cleanse me from all my sin;
3 *I acknowledge my transgressions;*
I see them o'er and o'er again.

4 *Against You only have I sinned,*
And done this evil in Your sight,
That speaking You'll be justified,
And be clear when You set things right.

5 *Behold I was shaped in iniquity,*
And in sin I was conceived;
6 *In the inward parts truth is desired,*
And You cannot be deceived.

In my hidden heart give me wisdom.
7 *Purge me and I'll be clean,*
Wash me, I'll be whiter than snow;
No longer will my sins be seen.

8 *Make me to hear joy and gladness,*
That broken bones may rejoice again,
9 *Lord, blot out all my iniquities;*
Hide Your face from all my sin.

10 *Renew a right spirit within me,*
Oh God, in me create a new heart.
11 *Do not cast me from Your presence,*
Let not Your Spirit from me depart.

12 *Unto me restore the joy of*
Your salvation which I once had;
Uphold me with a willing spirit,
As you did when I was a lad. ✝

Joshua 24:1-8; 15-17a

1 *Joshua gathered the people to Shechem.*
The elders, leaders and judges came
To present themselves before the Lord,
As obedient servants for Him to claim.

2 *Joshua said unto the people,*
"The Lord your God says this to you,
'Your ancestors lived beyond the river,
There they worshiped other gods too.

"'Terah, father of Abraham, lived there,
Who was also the father of Nahor.
I took Abraham from that land to
Canaan where he'd not been before.

3 *"'Through Canaan I led Abraham,*
Providing for his every need;
I gave him through Isaac many sons,
I promised Canaan to his seed.

4 *"'To Isaac I gave Jacob and Esau,*
To Esau the land round Mount Seir.
Jacob and his children to Egypt went,
And for many years they dwelled there.

5 *"'Unto you, I sent Moses and Aaron,*
And caused the plagues to come about
After doing this to the Egyptians,
From their land I brought you out.

6 *"'From Egypt I brought your fathers,*
Led you to the shore of the Red Sea;
When Egyptians pursued with their army,
Your fathers cried out unto Me.

7 *"'When your fathers cried for help,*
I brought darkness upon the land;
Placed it 'tween you and the Egyptians,
And protected you with My hand.

"'After you passed through the waters,
I covered the Egyptians with the sea,
Your eyes saw what I did to them there,
When from Egypt you did flee.

"'After being in the wilderness many years,
8 I brought you to the land of the Amorite.
There on the other side of the Jordan
They arose and against you did fight.

"'From before you, I destroyed them,
And I gave them into your hand.
They had not the power to defeat Me,
Now you possess their land.'

15 "If serving the Lord pleases not,
Then this day you must make a choice:
Will you serve the Lord, your God,
Will you obey only His voice?

"Or will you serve your fathers' gods,
Gods they served beyond the river,
Or serve the gods of Amorites,
Whose land to you God did deliver?

"But as for me and for my house,
The Lord is the God we will serve;
For He alone is the true God,
The One who can our lives preserve."

16 "God forbid," the people said,
"That the Lord we should ever forsake,
To go and serve those pagan gods,
Or other gods we could make.

17 "For the Lord who brought our fathers
Out of bondage from Egypt's land;
He did great wonders in our sight,
And kept us with His mighty hand." ✝

Ruth 1:1-11, 14-17

1 *In the days in which the judges ruled*
There was a famine in Israel.
A certain man from Bethlehem-Judah
Took his family to Moab to dwell.

2 *The man was called Elimelech,*
And Naomi was his wife's name;
Their sons were Mahlon and Chilion,
Into the land of Moab they came.

3 *While living in Moab, the father died,*
Naomi's sons were both left in her care.
4 *Each of them married a Moabite girl,*
And with them their life did share.

One son's bride was named Orpah, and
Ruth was the other son's wife;
They lived in Moab for ten years,
With Naomi shared their life.

5 *When Mahlon and Chilion died,*
Their mother felt all alone,
She chose to return to her homeland, and
Be with kin she once had known.

6 *She'd heard God had visited the land,*
And that the famine now was o'er.
7 *She arose with her daughters-in law,*
To go back where she'd lived before.

8 *Said she to her Moabite daughters-in-law,*
"To your mothers you should return,
You were kind to me when my sons were alive,
Now I'm no longer your concern.

9 *"May the Lord grant rest; may you*
Marry again and raise a family."
She kissed them and all of them wept,
Then Naomi said, "Depart from me."

10 They said, "Our place is with you.
To your homeland, we'll go too."
11 She replied, "Return my daughters,
I have no sons left for you."

14 They lifted their voices and wept again,
Then Orpah kissed Naomi and returned,
But Ruth held on to her
    mother-in-law,
For her, she was greatly concerned.

15 Naomi said, "Ruth, Orpah has gone,
To her people and gods she's returned.
Now you go after your sister-in-law,
A chance for new life you've earned."

16 Then Ruth said, "Don't urge me to
    leave you,
Or to stop following you as well.
For wherever you go, I will go
And where you live, I too will dwell.

"Your people shall be my people,
Also your God shall be my God.
17 Wherever you die, I will die
And I'll rest beneath the same sod.

"May the Lord God of Israel
With me deal most severely
If I allow anything save death
To separate you from me. ✝

1 Corinthians 15:50-58

50 *This I say to you, flesh and blood*
God's kingdom can't inherit,
Neither can the fleeting receive
What has everlasting merit.

51 *A mystery I now will show you*
Of this I'd have you know:
Not all of us shall sleep in death,
We'll all be changed to go...

52 *In the twinkling of an eye, when*
The last trumpet blast will sound,
The dead will rise incorruptible
Changed so no sin is found.

53 *We all must wear what never dies,*
The mortal, immortality.

54 *When this is done we then can say,*
"Death's swallowed up in victory.

55 *"Oh grave, where is your victory?*
Oh death, where is your bite?"
56 *Death's sting is sin, and so the law*
Gives sin its power and might.

57 *But thanks be unto our great God*
Who through Christ gives victory.
58 *Stand fast, brothers, in all you do*
From doing right let not move thee.

Give yourselves fully to God's work,
Your labor won't be in vain.
Continue in the Lord's service,
His labor you must maintain. ✝

2 Samuel 22:1-4, 19-25

1 *This is the song that David sang*
When the Lord delivered him from his foes,
And saved him from the hand of Saul
To follow the Lord, David chose.

2 *"The Lord is my rock and my fortress.*
The Lord is my deliverer too.
3 *The Lord, my rock, in Him will I trust;*
I'll serve Him in all that I do.

"He is my shield, my horn of salvation,
My high tower, refuge, Savior.
He's saved me from enemy acts,
And looked on me with great favor.

4 *"I will always call on the Lord,*
The One who is worthy of praise;
And I will be saved from my enemies,
I'll walk by His side all my days.

19 *"Enemies made my day a calamity, but*
God protected me with His might;
20 *He brought me forth into a large place,*
Because in me He did delight.

21 *"He rewarded me according to righteousness,*
By cleanness of hands He rewarded me;
22 *For I have kept the ways of the Lord,*
I have done nothing wickedly.

23 *"All of His judgments were before me.*
From His statutes I did not depart.
24 *I was always upright before Him*
I have kept iniquity from my heart.

"I have kept myself from iniquity.
25 *I've been repaid for my righteousness;*
Since I was clean before the Lord's eye
The Lord will care for me and bless." ✞

49

Isaiah 11:1-12

1 *A branch shall come from Jesse's roots,*
From his stem will come a rod,
2 *Upon this One shall come and rest*
The Spirit of our holy God.

The Spirit of wisdom and understanding,
The Spirit of counsel will appear;
He'll have knowledge and have might,
And Jehovah God He will fear.

3 *The Spirit will give Him understanding,*
For it's Jehovah God He fears,
He'll not judge after what He sees,
Nor reprove after what He hears.

4 *With righteousness He will judge the*
poor,
With fairness He'll reprove the meek.

With the rod of His mouth He'll
smite the earth,
And bring justice unto the weak.

He'll slay the wicked with His breath,
5 *Faithfulness shall girdle His reins,*
Righteousness shall be about His waist,
He will remove sin's condemning stains.

6 *The wolf shall dwell in peace with the*
lamb,
The goat abide with the leopard wild,
The young lion together with the yearling,
They will be led by a child.

7 *The cow and bear shall feed together,*
Their young ones lie down with one another,
The lion shall eat straw like the ox,
And one will not harm the other.

8 *The suckling child shall play upon the hole*
Of the adder and not be hurt;
The weaned child shall play in the serpent's den;
Yet its bite he will avert.

9 *It shall come to pass in My holy mountain*
That no destruction or hurt you'll see;
For the earth shall be full of the knowledge of God,
As the waters that cover the sea.

10 *A root of Jesse shall reign that day,*
For the people He will be a banner,
And unto Him shall the Gentiles flock;
His rest will be glorious in manner.

11 *It shall come to pass on that great day,*
That the Lord shall again set His hand
To recover a remnant of His chosen people,
And return them to their land.

They'll return from Assyria and Egypt;
From Pathros they'll come back home.
From Cush, Elam, Shinar and Hamath,
And from the islands never to roam.

12 *He shall hang up a banner for the nations,*
Israel's outcasts will have new birth;
He'll gather together the dispersed of Judah
From the four corners of earth. ✞

Psalm 149

1 *Sing a new song to the Lord,*
Let His saints unto Him sing,
2 *Let all Israel rejoice in God,*
And be joyful in their King.

3 *Let them praise the Lord with dance,*
And with harp and timbrel too.
4 *For the Lord enjoys His people,*
If to Him they will be true.

He will beautify the meek,
Unto them He'll bring salvation,
For our Lord is all sufficient,
In the hardest situation.

5 *Let the saints find joy in glory,*
Let them sing upon their bed,
Let them honor the Lord our God,
For by Him they will be fed.

6 *Let them praise Him with their mouth,*
And a sword within their hand;
7 *They will execute God's judgment*
On the heathen in the land.

8 *They'll bind their kings with fetters,*
And their nobles with a chain,
9 *Carrying out God's written judgment,*
Honor for His saints they'll gain. †

James 1:2-11

2 *Consider it joy my brethren*
When trials on you are loosed.
3 *Know that by testing of your faith*
Patience will be produced.

4 *Let patience have its result, that you*
May be perfect and complete,
And that you may lack for nothing,
In all you will be replete.

5 *If any of you lacks wisdom*
Then let him God approach,
He gives to all generously —
He gives without reproach.

6 *But when he asks, he must believe,*
Without having any doubt.

The one who doubts is like the surf,
By the wind it's tossed about.

7 *That man who doubts should not expect*
From God anything he'll receive.
8 *He's double-minded and unstable*
In what he does and believes.

9 *Let those of humble circumstance,*
Take pride in their high station
10 *But the rich should take pride in*
Their lowly situation,

For he'll pass away like flowers.
11 *The sun rises with scorching heat,*
And withers the plant; its blooms fall
For its beauty it does defeat. ✞

Jonah 1:15, 17; 2:1-10

15 *Jonah was on a ship running from God,*
When sailors threw him in the sea;
17 *A great fish the Lord had prepared*
Swallowed Jonah while he tried to flee.

2:1 *There Jonah prayed unto Jehovah,*
From the big fish in the sea,
2 *He cried from the depths of Sheol,*
And the Lord heard his earnest plea:

3 *"You cast me into the briny deep;*
The raging sea tossed me about.
Billows and waves passed over me,
I was lost, of that I had no doubt.

4 *"Lord, You cast me out of Your sight,*
Will I ever see Your temple again?

5 *The weeds are wrapped around my head,*
And the depths now close me in.

6 *"I plunged to the roots of the mountains*
That descend deep into the ocean cup.
The earth with its bars closed over me,
Yet from the pit, Jehovah brought me up.

7 *"I remembered the Lord when I fainted;*
In Your temple, my prayer went to You;
8 *If I regard vanities I reject mercy,*
9 *But I'll pay the vows that are due.*

"Salvation comes only from Jehovah,
Mercy comes to me from His hand."
10 *Hearing this, the Lord spoke to the fish,*
And it vomited Jonah to dry land. ♱

1 Kings 3:5-14

5 The Lord appeared to Solomon in Gibeon.
He spoke to him in a dream at night.
He said, "Ask what you want from Me;
You have found favor in My sight."

6 Said Solomon, "Great mercy and kindness
To my father You have made known.
Because of his truth and uprightness,
You gave him a son upon his throne.

7 "Now Lord, I'm king instead of my father,
I feel just like a little child.
I don't know how to go out or come in.
Burdens of government on me are piled.

8 "You put me in the midst of a great people,
A people which for Yourself You've chosen;
They are so many, they cannot be counted.
Their needs are great, as You've known.

9 "Give to me understanding, so
I may discern between bad and good;
Who can judge so great a multitude,
Teach them to do the things they should?"

10 Solomon's request pleased God greatly,
11 God said, "Since you've asked this thing,
You've not asked for long life or riches,
Or victory over your enemies to bring.

"You've asked for understanding to judge.
This people in the land where you dwell.
12 Behold, I have given what you requested,
13 Wisdom, riches and honor as well.

"Among kings there'll be none like you,
14 And if you always walk in my ways,
Keep My commands as did your father,
Then I will surely lengthen your days." ✞

Acts 1:1-11

1 *The former book I made for you*
Oh Theophilus, my friend,
About all that Jesus did and taught,
From beginning to the end.

2 *From the day He came to the earth*
Until He rose to heaven,
After that through the Spirit, He
Gave orders to His chosen.

3 *To these He showed himself alive-*
A total of forty days,
He spoke to them concerning God
He did this in many ways.

4 *Having assembled them, Jesus said,*
"Jerusalem don't leave,
But wait for the Father's promise, which
I said you would receive.

5 *"For John baptized with water, yet*
By the Spirit you'll baptized be;
It'll happen to you a few days hence
When the Spirit comes upon thee."

6 *So when they came together, they*
Asked, "Lord could this be the day
That You'll restore the kingdom?
Tell us before going away."

7 He said, "You need not know the times,
Nor need you know the seasons,
The Father keeps these to Himself
For this He has His reasons.

8 "But you'll receive great power when
The Spirit comes upon you.
You all shall be My witnesses
In whatever you say and do.

"First to Jerusalem and then,
To Judea you must go,
Samaria and the whole world,
My message all must know."

9 Done speaking, He was lifted up,
While His disciples looked on;
A cloud received Him from their sight;
Into the sky He'd gone...

10 As they gazed up into the sky
With their eyes still open wide,
Two men in white clothing came
And stood there by their side.

11 They said, "You men of Galilee
Why look you at the sky?
This Jesus, taken from heaven shall
Come again from on high." ✝

57

1 Samuel 16:1-13

1 The Lord called Samuel and unto him said,
"Why do you still mourn over Saul?
I've rejected him, fill your horn with oil,
A new king for Israel I'll call.

"I'm sending you to the Bethlehemite,
From his sons I will choose a new king."
2 Samuel replied, "How can I go there
now,
If Saul hears of it, death he'll bring."

"Take a heifer with you," said the
Lord.
3 "Call Jesse to come meet with you.
Tell him you've come to sacrifice,
And I'll show you what you're to do.

"There you'll anoint the one I name."
4 So Samuel took the heifer to Bethlehem.

The town leaders said, "Do you come
in peace?"
His coming had brought fear on them.

5 Samuel said, "Yes, I come in peace;
A sacrifice to the Lord, I'm to make.
Sanctify yourselves and come with me.
In the offering I'd have you partake."

He sanctified Jesse and his sons
And he called them to the sacrifice.
6 When they arrived he looked at Eliab,
And thought, "This young man looks nice.

"Surely the Lord's anointed is before me."
7 But the Lord said, "Don't look on
his face,
And don't look on the height of his stature,
In My choice these have no place.

"The Lord doesn't see man as man
    does see,
But man only sees man in part,
On the outward appearance he does look,
But the Lord looks in man's heart."

8 Jesse presented Abinadab to Samuel
    who said,
"I know God hasn't chosen this son."
9 Then Jesse had Shammah pass before
    Samuel,
Who said, "Neither has He chose this one."

10 Seven of Jesse's sons came before
    Samuel.
Samuel said, "The Lord has chosen none.
11 Have I seen all of your children,
Do you not have another son?"

"The youngest is tending the sheep,"
    Jesse said.
Samuel replied, "Go, have him brought
    in.
We won't sit down until he arrives,
Until he comes the sacrifice won't begin."

12 So they sent for David and had him
    come;
He was tanned and a handsome young man.
God said to Samuel, "Anoint this boy.
He'll be king, for this is my plan."

13 Then Samuel took the horn of oil,
Anointed David in the midst of his
    brothers,
And the Spirit of the Lord came on David,
From that day forward to all others. ✝

Psalm 56

1 *Be merciful to me, O God,*
My enemies would swallow me I fear;
Their fighting daily torments me,
But Your goodness brings me cheer.

2 *I face my enemies every day,*
And against me many fight,
But I pray to You, Most High,
To save me by Your might.

3 *Whenever I am much afraid,*
I will put my trust in You;
I know that You can save me,
No matter what my foes may do.

4 *Unto God I'll give my praise,*
And in Him I'll put my trust;
I'll not fear what flesh can do,
For I know my God is just.

5 *Every day they twist my words,*
Trapping me in what I say.
They think evil thoughts of me,
And they try to block my way.

6 *Often they all meet together,*
And hide along my path;
They mark my steps, wait for my soul;
How can I escape their wrath?

7 *Shall they escape by iniquity?*
O God, in anger cast them down,
Bring their evil plans to naught,
And thus glorify Your crown.

8 *O Lord, You know my wanderings,*
You know the path I have trod.
All my tears You have bottled up;
Are they not in the Book of God?

9 *And when I cry unto You, Lord,*
My enemies will turn back.
This I know for God is with me,
Therefore, I'll have no lack.

10 *I will give praise to God's Word,*
11 *I will put my trust in God,*
I will not fear what man can do,
While on this earth I trod.

12 *I will perform my vows, O God,*
I will render all praise to You,
13 *For You have saved my soul from death,*
In spite of what My foes could do.

You will keep my feet from falling,
That I may walk before my God;
In the blessed land of the living,
I'll receive Your approving nod. ✝

1 Samuel 17:38-50a

38 *Saul clothed David with his own*
  armor,
Put a brass helmet upon his head;
39 *Dressed in armor, a sword at his side,*
He couldn't move and he felt like lead.

David said to Saul, "I can't use these
  things,
I've never worn such armor before.
If I wore these I could not move,
Before starting, the fight would be o'er."

40 *David shed the armor, took his*
  staff in hand,
Grabbed five smooth stones from a brook.
He put these stones in his shepherd bag;
His sling with him he also took.

Then David started toward the Philistine,
41 *And the Philistine to David drew near,*
His armor bearer strutting before him,
In the giant there seemed no fear.

42 *Upon seeing David he cursed in*
  contempt,
For he saw David was just a lad.
43 *He said, "Am I a dog that you come*
  with a stick?
Has Israel sent the best they had?

44 *"I'll feed your flesh to the fowls of*
  the air,
The beasts of the field will feast on you."
45 *David said, "You come against me*
  with a sword,
You're bearing a shield and a spear too.

"But I come to you in the name of the
    Lord,
The Lord of hosts, Israel's God.
This is the One you've defied and cursed.
Soon He'll place you 'neath the sod.

46 "The Lord will give you into my hand;
I will smite you and cut off your head.
Many more Philistines will die this day
By their bodies fowls will be fed.

"The beasts of the earth will also feed.
Israel's God the whole world will know;
47 The Lord doesn't save by sword and
    spear;
But those trusting Him defeat their foe."

48 The giant moved out and came to
    meet David,
49 David stepped forward and slung a
    stone.
The stone pierced the forehead of
    Goliath the giant,
Hitting hard, it went clear through
    the bone.

The Philistine buckled and fell to the
    earth;
Golilath's face was down in the dust;
50 Little David prevailed o'er the
    mocker of God,
Because in God he had put his trust. ✞

Romans 5:1-10

1 *Being justified by faith,*
With God we now have peace.
Through Jesus Christ our Lord
This peace will never cease.

2 *We now have access to Him*
By faith into this grace
Where we stand in hope of glory,
When we see the heavenly place.

3 *We rejoice in our suffering,*
For suffering makes our patience strong,
4 *And patience produces experience*
Experience, hope, that gives us a song.

5 *This hope does not disappoint us*
Because God's love is poured out;
Through the Holy Spirit is given
Grace to take away all doubt.

6 *For while we were without strength,*
Christ showed us that He cared.
He came and gave His life for us,
He died, His love to share.

7 *To die for a righteous man is rare,*
For a good man some have dared.
8 *While sinners yet, Christ died for us*
By His death His love He shared.

9 *From God's wrath we have been saved;*
Through His blood we're justified,
10 *For while we were yet sinners,*
Jesus came and for us died.

Thus reconciled to God through Christ
From all our sin and strife,
Much more having been reconciled
Shall we be saved by His life. ✝

2 Kings 20:1-7

1 *Hezekiah the king became sick unto death.*
The prophet Isaiah came to him and said,
"Thus says the Lord: Put your house in order,
For in a short while you will be dead."

2 *Hezekiah turned his face to the wall.*
3 *"Remember, Lord how I walked before You?*
In Your truth and with a perfect heart,
I've done the things You wanted me to do."

Then Hezekiah bowed his head and cried.
4 *And before Isaiah reached the middle court*
The Lord spoke and said to the prophet,
5 *"Return to Hezekiah; I've changed*
    My report.

"Say: The God of David, your father
Has seen your tears and heard your prayer.
I will heal you and three days from now
You shall go to My house and worship there.

6 *"I'll add to your life fifteen years,*
And I'll deliver you from the Assyrian king.
I'll defend your land for My own sake,
And for David's sake victory I'll bring."

7 *Isaiah said, "Take a lump of figs.*
Make a paste and spread it on the boil."
Thus from his sickness Hezekiah
    recovered,
And the death angel the Lord did foil. ☦

Daniel 5:30,31; 6:1-23

30 *On the very night Belshazzar was killed,*
31 *Darius the Mede succeeded to the throne,*
6:1 *He appointed a hundred and twenty princes,*
2 *Over the princes three presidents strong.*

One president was Daniel from the old regime,
3 *Darius took note of his spirit and skill,*
The king made him first of the three presidents,
Because he was able and a man of good will.

4 *The jealous officials sought to find something*
To bring charges against Daniel to the king,

But no fault or error could they find against him,
For he was trustworthy in everything.

5 *The plotters said, "We shall find nothing Against Daniel with the king we can share, Unless it is something about his God, With whom he spends much time in prayer."*

6 *Together one day they approached the king.*
They said, "May you, O king forever live,
7 *The presidents, princes and other officials Have met and this advice we would give:*

"Make a decree that for thirty days, An order that will apply to all men, If anyone petitions ought but you, He shall be cast into the lions' den.

8 *"Now, O king, sign this decree,*
Sign it for your honor's sake,
And in the law of the Medes and
Persians,
No change can anyone make."

9 *King Dairus signed the law they asked.*
10 *When Daniel heard of the decree,*
He opened his windows toward
Jerusalem
And there presented to God his plea.

Three times a day Daniel gave thanks
and prayed;
Praise and petitions he did bring.
11 *Men rushed to his house and found*
him praying,
To his God and not to the king.

12 *They returned and said, "Did you, O king,*
Issue a decree and sign it too:
For thirty days no petition be made
To any god or man but you?

"If this decree someone should not heed,
Would casting to the lions be his lot?"
The king answered, "Yes, this is true.
The Medes' and Persians' law altereth
not."

13 *"O king, this Daniel," they said,*
"Does not regard the words you say,
He pays no attention to your decree,
Prays three times to his God each day."

14 *Now when the king did hear these words,*
He was grieved for what he had done.
He sought some way to save Daniel,
He labored 'til setting of the sun.

15 *At evening the men reminded the king,*
"The law of the Persians and Medes
Says this decree cannot be changed,
Daniel must pay for his deeds."

16 *The king ordered that Daniel be brought,*
Said, "By the law, this I must do,
Into the den of lions have you cast;
May the God you serve deliver you."

17 *A stone was put on the den's mouth,*
With the king's own ring it was sealed;
He sealed it with the ring of state,
To prove the law had not been repealed.

18 *The king turned and went back to*
*   his palace,*
There he fasted the whole night through,
No music was played for him that evening,
And sleep did depart from him too.

19 *Early the next morning the king arose,*
And hurried to the lions' den;
20 *In a breaking voice, he cried, "O Daniel!"*
Then he called Daniel's name again.

"The living God whom you do serve,
Has He come and delivered you?
Has He spared you from the hungry lions,
As I hoped that He would do?"

21 *Daniel replied, "O king, live forever,*
22 *God heard me when I did call.*
He sent an angel and shut their mouths,
And they hurt me not at all."

23 *Then the king was very happy,*
From the den he had Daniel brought out.
No hurt or scratch was found upon him,
For his God he did not doubt. ✞

Proverbs 2:1-11

1 *My son, if you'll receive My words;*
Hide My commands in your mind,
2 *Inclining your ear to wisdom,*
An understanding heart you'll find.

3 *If you cry out after knowledge,*
Lift your voice to understand,
4 *If you seek knowledge as silver*
And to it lift up your hand,

If you seek it as a hidden treasure
5 *You'll understand the fear of the Lord.*
Then you'll find the knowledge of God;
This will be your great reward.

6 *It is the Lord who gives wisdom, with*
Knowledge and understanding in His talk.
7 *He lays up wisdom for the righteous,*
A shield to those who rightly walk.

8 *The Lord gives good sense to the godly,*
His saints, their way He'll preserve.
9 *He shows how to make right decisions,*
And make judgment that does not swerve.

10 *When wisdom enters your heart,*
You'll find your joy will be whole.
11 *Then discretion shall protect you*
And understanding will guard your soul. ✝

1 Peter 1:2b-13

2b *May grace and peace come to you, and*
Be yours in fullest measure,
May His blessings fall on you, may
His service be your treasure.

3 *Blessed be the God and Father, who*
Sent Christ to dwell with men;
Who according to His great mercy
Let us be born again.

We now have a living hope, through Christ's
Resurrection from the dead,
4 *To obtain an inheritance for us*
Which cannot then be shed.

It's imperishable, undefiled,
It will not fade away,
Reserved for you in heaven above,
At God's great judgment day.

5 *We are protected by God's power.*
Through faith, salvation's sealed.
When the last times appear, it will
Be ready to be revealed.

6 *By this you should rejoice, although*
Now for a little while
You may have to be distressed by
Various and sundry trial.

7 *The genuineness of your faith*
Is God's foremost desire,
It is more precious than pure gold
Which is tested by the fire.

May your faith result in glory to God,
May loud your voices raise,
At the revelation of Jesus Christ
Give Him honor and praise.

8 *Though you haven't seen Him in person,*
You love Him, this I know.
And though you don't see Him now, He
Sets your spirits aglow.

But because you believe in Him,
You all greatly rejoice.
Your joy is inexpressible,
To Him lift up your voice.

9 *As to your faith's outcome, you'll get*
Salvation of your soul
Through your faith in Christ Jesus,
   through
Whose strength you've been made whole.

10 *And as to this salvation, those*
Who prophesied such to thee
Of the grace that was to come made
Careful search and inquiry;

11 *They sought to know what time He'd come,*
What kind of man He'd be.
Christ's Spirit in them indicated
He'd die upon a tree.

12 *They told of glories soon to come.*
To them, they were revealed.
They did not serve themselves, but to
You, these things they appealed.

Through those who have preached the
   gospel, these
Things have been announced to you;
Sent from heaven by the Spirit, things
Which angels would look into.

13 *So gird your minds, be sober, fix*
Your hope upon the grace
Which will come unto you when you
Will see Christ face to face. ✝

Psalm 139:1-12

1 *Lord, You search and truly know me,*
2 *When I sit and when I rise,*
My thoughts you know when far away,
You always know where my heart lies.

3 *You know where I walk and sleep,*
You are aware of my every way,
4 *You know what my tongue will utter,*
You know everything I'll say.

5 *You are before me and behind me,*
On me You have placed Your hand;
6 *Such knowledge is too great for me,*
And too high to understand.

7 *From Your Spirit I can't escape,*
From Your presence I cannot flee.

8 *If I should ascend to heaven*
I know that there, You would be.

If I make my bed with the dead,
Behold, I would find You there.
There is no place for me to hide,
For Your Spirit is everywhere.

9 *If I take the wings of morning,*
And dwell far out in the sea,
10 *Even there shall your hand lead me,*
For Your right hand strong shall be.

11 *If I'm covered by the darkness,*
Where the night shall be as light,
12 *Darkness cannot hide me from You,*
For Your darkness shall be bright. ✝

Ephesians 6:11 - 20

11 *Put on the full armor of God,*
So that you may stand strong
Against all of the devil's schemes
Which lead you into wrong.

12 *Our struggle isn't against flesh, but*
Against rulers and powers,
Against the darkness, which even
In heavenly places towers.

13 *Take God's full armor, so that you*
Can resist on the evil day,
And having done all, can stand firm
When evil comes your way.

14 *Stand firm, loins girded with truth, don*
The breastplate of righteousness,

15 *Your feet shod with the gospel, be*
Prepared Christ to confess.

16 *Take up the shield of faith, the missiles*
Of the evil one put out.

17 *Then take the helmet of salvation,*
Wear it to remove any doubt.

And take up the sword of the Spirit,
Which is God's holy Word.

18 *Pray patiently for all the saints*
That no harm will be incurred,

19 *And that with boldness, I'll proclaim*
The gospel's mystery,

20 *For which I'm an ambassador,*
Although in chains I be. ✝

Philippians 2:5-15

5 *The attitude which was in Christ*
Let it be found in thee.
6 *Being in nature, God, He*
Didn't scorn equality.

7 *Instead, Christ made Himself nothing*
As a man, a servant became.
8 *Found as a man, humbled Himself,*
Died on a cross to bear our shame.

9 *Therefore, God hath exalted Him,*
With honor and highest fame,
Also on Him bestowed
A name above every name.

10 *That at the name of Jesus Christ*
Every knee should bow low,
Of all who dwell in heaven fair;
On earth, or those below.

11 *And so every tongue shall then confess*
That Jesus Christ is the Lord,
To the glory of God the Father,
12 *As you've obeyed in one accord.*

Not only when you are in my presence
But when I'm away from you,
Continue to work out your salvation
With fear and trembling too.

13 *For it's God who's at work in you,*
By His purpose to will and act.
14 *Do all things without complaining,*
No arguing or talking back.

15 *So that you become blameless and pure,*
Like the children of God you are.
In a crooked, deprived generation,
In which you shine like a star. ✝

Ecclesiastes 3:1-11

1 *Everything has a time and season,*
A time for every purpose under the sun.
2 *A time to be born, a time to die,*
A time to walk, a time to run.

A time to plant, a time to pluck,
For the harvest will surely come.
3 *A time to kill, a time to heal,*
A time to talk, a time to be mum,

A time to break down, a time to build up,
4 *A time to laugh, a time to weep,*
A time to mourn, a time to dance,
5 *A time to scatter stones, a time to keep.*

A time to embrace, a time to refrain,
6 *A time to get, a time to lose,*

A time to keep, a time to cast away,
A time to reach out, a time to refuse,

7 *A time to rend, and a time to sew,*
A time to keep silent, and a time to speak,
8 *A time to love, a time to hate,*
A time for war, a time peace to seek.

9 *What profit has he who works very hard?*
He labors all day and what does he get?
10 *I have seen the travail given by God,*
He has no choice but to strive in it.

11 *All that is beautiful God has made.*
He sets eternity in our hearts.
No one can fathom the work of God
Where it will end, or where it starts. ✝

Acts 3:1-16

1 Peter and John went to the temple
At the ninth hour of prayer.
2 A certain man, crippled from birth,
Every day was carried there.

They left him at the temple gate,
Called Beautiful by name,
To beg from all who entered there
Who to the temple came.

3 He saw Peter and John coming,
Money he asked to receive.
4 Peter and John gazed right at him,
Said, "Look at us and believe."

5 He gave them his total attention,
Listened as he'd been told.
6 Peter leaned down and said to the man,
"I've no silver or gold.

"But what I have, I give to thee
Better than silver and gold.
In Jesus' name, rise and walk, for
Through Him is healing untold."

7 Peter seized him by the right hand
And raised him up to his feet.
Strength flowed into the beggar's legs
As he stood upon the street.

8 With a leap he stood upright, and
He began to jump and shout.
To the temple walked praising
God for what had come about.

9 All the people saw him walking,
Shouting praises to God; for he
10 Was the one they'd seen at the gate,
Lame and begging, but now set free.

11 *While he clung to the apostles,*
All the people stood amazed,
They came running up to that place,
Called Solomon's Colonnade.

12 *The people came and crowded 'round*
To see and hear them talk.
Said Peter, "Why do you marvel?
I didn't make him walk.

13 *"The God of Abraham and Isaac,*
And of Jacob our father, too,
Has glorified his servant Jesus,
Who was delivered up by you.

"Whom you disowned in Pilate's presence,
Pilate wanted His release,
14 *You asked instead for a murderer*
And denied the Prince of Peace.

15 *"You put to death the Author of Life,*
Whom God raised from the dead,
A fact we all are witnesses of,
And by Him we are led.

16 *"His faith came through Jesus, when*
On Him he did call;
He has been given perfect health
In the prescence of us all." ✝

77

Philippians 1:2-11

2 *Grace and peace to you from our God*
And our Lord Jesus, too.
3 *I thank God in all things, 'specially*
My remembrance of you.

4 *I always make these prayers with joy,*
When I remember how
5 *You've always shared the gospel from*
The first day until now.

6 *I'm confident of this that God's*
Good work begun in you
He will perfect until the day
When Christ returns anew.

7 *It's right for me to feel this way*
Because you're in my heart,
You've shared my imprisonment, in
God's grace you've had a part.

8 *For God is my witness who knows*
How much I long for you,
With all the love of Jesus Christ
Your faces I would view.

9 *And this is my prayer for you daily,*
That your love continues to grow,
Both in all your judgement
And in what you know.

10 *So that you may approve things that*
Are good in every way,
That you be sincere and blameless 'til
The coming of Christ's day.

11 *Having been filled with the fruit of*
God's holy righteous ways,
Which comes through Jesus Christ unto
God's glory and His praise. ✝

Proverbs 3:1-10

1 *My son, forget not my law;*
And keep My commands is my plea;
2 *For length of days and long life,*
And peace they shall add to thee.

3 *Let mercy and truth forsake you not,*
Bind them around your neck;
Write them on the table of your heart; for
Wrong ways they will check.

4 *You will find favor with God and man*
A good name will be your reward,
And from you God will not depart
As you pay heed to His Word.

5 *Trust in the Lord with all your heart,*
To your understanding, do not lean.
6 *In all your ways acknowledge Him,*
So His directions can be seen.

7 *Be not wise in your own eyes;*
Fear the Lord, let not evil be known.
8 *It will be as health unto your navel,*
And be as marrow to your bone.

9 *Honor the Lord with your substance and*
The first fruits of your increase;
10 *So shall your barns be overflowing,*
The wine of blessings will not cease. ✞

Isaiah 6:1-8

1 *The year that King Uzziah died*
I saw the Lord on a throne.
I saw Him high and lifted up.
In fear, I could only groan.

For His train filled all the temple,
2 *And above it stood seraphim high,*
Two wings over the feet and face of each,
Two more helped each one fly.

3 *One seraphim cried to another:*
"Holy, holy, holy, the Lord of hosts:
The earth is full of His glory
And it reaches around all the coasts."

4 *The posts of the door did move*
At the voice of him that cried,
And the house was filled with holy smoke,
There was no place I could hide.

5 *Then said I, "Woe is me,*
I'm a man with lips unclean.
The people with whom I dwell
Are sinful, this is easy seen.

" For my eyes have seen the King,
The Lord of hosts, God of our land."
6 *Then a seraphim flew to me*
With a live coal in his hand.

He'd taken it from the altar;
7 *It touched my mouth, my spirit surged.*
I heard him say, "This touched your lips,
Your iniquity's gone, your sin is purged."

8 *Then I heard the Lord's voice saying:*
"Whom shall I send, who will go?"
And I said, "Here am I, send me."
"Yes! Tell these people. Bravo!" ✝

Romans 12:1-7

1 *I beseech you, therefore, brothers,*
By God's mercy and His love,
To present your bodies a living
Sacrifice to our God above.

This is your holy service.
2 *To this world be not conformed,*
But by renewing of your mind
You will know you are transformed.

That you may prove the will of God
And the Lord's wisdom perfect.
Live, then, as God would have you live
And in all things be correct.

3 *For through the grace that's given me*
I say this to each of you,
Don't think more highly of yourself
Than you really ought to do;

But think you clearly, for to each
Some faith the Lord does allot
4 *The body's parts are many, but*
The same function they have not.

5 *So we, who are many people,*
In Christ we have become one.
We're members one of another
Through Jesus Christ, God's Son.

6 *And having gifts that differ,*
Given according to God's grace.
Let us use them accordingly
And for Jesus take our place.

If your gift is prophecy,
Prophesy by faith given thee.
7 *Or if your gift is serving, then*
Serve Christ with integrity. ✝

Ephesians 2:6-22

6 *He raised us up with Him and put*
Us in the heavenly place,
This in Christ Jesus, because of
His mercy and His grace.

7 *That in ages to come He might*
Show exceeding riches of grace,
When in kindness toward us in Christ
We stand before His face.

8 *For by grace you have been saved, this*
Is God's own holy gift,
You can do nothing of yourself,
Your sins you cannot shift.

9 *Salvation does not come from works,*
Therefore, no one should boast.
It is a gift that comes from God,
The great and heavenly Host.

10 *Created in Christ for good works,*
We are God's workmanship,
Which God beforehand did ordain,
From which we cannot slip.

11 *Remember, you who are Gentiles by birth*
Were called "uncircumcised" by those
Who call themselves "the circumcision"
Because they were from the family God chose.

12 *You will recall how at that time*
You were from Christ separated,
Excluded from Israel's covenant
And the promises that I've stated.

You were without God in the world,
Hopeless, you lived in fear,
13 *But now in the blood of Jesus Christ,*
To God you've been brought near.

14 *For He Himself is our peace, who*
Made both groups into one
And broke down the dividing wall
Through Jesus Christ, His Son,

15 *Having abolished fleshly law,*
And thus the enmity,
Contained in the ordinances which
Separated you from me.

To make the two become one, He'd
Thus establish peace
16 *And reconciled them both to God,*
Through the cross, strife would cease.

Thus enmity was put to death
17 *And to you peace was preached.*
Both those near and far away
By His peace have been reached.

18 *In one spirit with the Father, we*
Both to Him have access.
19 *Therefore, you are no longer strangers*
When Jesus you confess.

You are all citizens with the saints,
Dwelling within God's household,
20 *Built upon the foundation of apostles*
And the prophets of old.

Christ Himself is the cornerstone
21 *On whom the building rests,*
Fitted into a holy temple where
Christ as Lord is confessed.

22 *Into whom you are being built*
Along with fellow believers,
A dwelling place of God in Spirit
With all the grace receivers. ✝

Isaiah 53:1-8

1 *Who has believed our report?*
To whom is the Lord's arm known?
2 *He comes as a tender plant,*
As a root from dry ground grown.

He has no form or comeliness;
In Him no beauty we see,
Nothing in Him do we desire;
What kind of a person is He?

3 *He's despised and rejected of men;*
Man of sorrows, with grief as His lot;
We hid as it were our faces from Him;
He was despised; we esteemed Him not.

4 *Surely He has borne our griefs,*
And for us has been distressed;
Yet we considered Him stricken by God,
Smitten by God, and by man oppressed.

5 *For our transgressions, He was wounded,*
He was bruised for all our sin;
The chastisement of our peace was on Him;
His stripes made us whole again.

6 *All we like sheep have gone astray;*
Each has turned down his own path;
On Him God has laid our iniquity;
So we can escape God's wrath.

7 *He was oppressed, He was afflicted;*
Yet from His mouth He said not a word;
A lamb for slaughter, a sheep for shearing,
From His lips no protest was heard.

8 *Oppressed and judged, He was taken away.*
Who can speak of His posterity?
He was cut from the land of the living.
My people's transgression bore He. ✝

1 Corinthians 2:9-16

9 *So just as it has been written,*
No eye has seen, nor heard by ear
Or mind envisioned, what God has
Prepared for those who love Him dear.

10 *God showed them through His Spirit;*
For the Spirit finds all things,
Searching God's deepest thoughts, and
To us understanding brings.

11 *Aren't a man's thoughts known only*
By that man's spirit alone?
So, too, the thoughts of God are,
Only to His Spirit known.

12 *The world's spirit is not what*
Was given to you and me.
It's God's Spirit we've received
To grasp what He gave so free.

13 *We do not speak with words that are*
From human wisdom alone,
But words taught by the Spirit,
Truths only the Spirit has known.

14 *The natural man spurns these things;*
God's Spirit he can't understand.
To discern the things of God,
Spiritual sight He does demand.

15 *The spiritual man makes judgments,*
On whatever life will bring,
But he may not be judged, not by
Anyone or anything.

16 *For who has known the mind of God*
That he might instruct the Lord?
But the mind of Christ have we, who
Received God's wisdom outpoured. ✝

2 Corinthians 5:15-21

15 *He died for all, that those who live*
Live for themselves no longer,
But live for Him who died and rose,
And through Him are made stronger.

16 *Thus we recognize none of you*
By the views of folks today,
Though we once viewed Christ as they did,
We no longer see this way.

17 *Now if anyone be in Christ*
He's a new creature I've no doubt.
For old things have all passed away,
And now new things have come about.

18 *Each of these things are from the Lord,*
To Him we've been reconciled.
Through Jesus Christ, His only Son,
We have each become His child.

This ministry was given us,
Through Christ, who bought us back.
19 *Who reconciles us to Himself,*
Keeping of our sins no track.

He trusted to us the message,
Of reconciliation,
And calls on us to take His Word,
To those in every nation.

20 *So we are Christ's ambassadors,*
Portraying Him on this sod.
We beg you on behalf of Christ:
Be reconciled to God.

21 *God made the One who knew no sin*
That He be made sin for us,
That through Him we would then become
The Lord's holy righteousness. ♱

Galatians 2:15-21

15 *Our parents were not Gentiles, but*
We are descendants of the Jews
16 *We know that justification*
By the law we now refuse.

We're justified by faith in Christ,
Who for us came and died,
Not by works of the law, for by
Works none are justified.

17 *If while seeking to be justified*
We're found to sinners be,
Is Christ then a minister of sin?
No, this could never be.

18 *Should I rebuild what I destroyed*
A lawbreaker I prove to be,

19 *Through the law I died, so that I*
Might live for the Lord only.

20 *I have been crucified with Christ;*
It's no longer I who live,
But Jesus Christ who lives in me;
For myself to Him I give.

The life I live in the flesh, I live
By faith in God's true Son,
Who loved and gave Himself for me,
I'm glad for what He's done.

21 *I don't make void the grace of God*
That, I have not tried.
If righteousness comes through the law
Then Christ need not have died. ✞

Romans 8:23 - 39

23b *We wait eagerly to become*
Children of God by adoption,
And also stand in eager hope
Of our bodies' sure redemption.

24 *For in hope were we saved, but hope*
That's seen is hope no more.
One does not hope for what one sees,
For he knows what lies in store.

25 *If we hope for what we don't have,*
Then we with patience wait,
26 *Likewise, the Spirit helps us in*
Our weakness, I truly state.

When we don't know how to pray,
The Spirit, for us intercedes
With groanings far too deep for words,
To God the Spirit pleads.

27 *He who searches in our hearts*
Knows what's in the Spirit's mind,
Because He intercedes for saints
According to His will divine.

28 *We know all things work together*
For good to those who, in kind,
Love the Lord God and are called
According to what He designed.

29 *Those foreknown He planned that they*
Would bear the likeness of His Son;
First born of many brethren,
That His will might be done.

30 *Those He predestined, He also called;*
Those he called He justified,
Those He justified through the love
Of Christ, He also glorified.

31 *What shall we say to these things? If*
God's for us who can against us be?
32 *He who didn't spare His own Son but*
Delivered Him for you and me.

Since He will give all things to us,
33 *Who will accuse God's elect?*
God is the one who justifies,
And we are among the select.

34 *Who is he that condemns us?*
Christ died and He is risen again.
He now stands there at God's right hand
Interceding for our gain.

35 *Who'll separate us from Christ's love?*
Shall tribulation, or distress,
Shall persecution, or famine great,
Peril, sword, or nakedness?

36 *As it's written: For thy sake*
All day long we do face death;
We're considered sheep for slaughter, by
Those who'd stamp out our breath.

37 *Nay in all these things we conquer*
Through Him who loved us so.
38 *I'm certain neither death nor life*
Nor powers, angels, demons low,

No power can separate us.
39 *Neither depth nor elevation,*
Nor any creature anywhere
No matter what its station,

Can separate us from God's love
Found in Christ our risen Lord.
For He has saved and cleansed us,
Holding us by love's strong cord. ✝

Jeremiah 18:1-10

1 *To Jeremiah came this word of the Lord,*
2 *Saying, "Go down to the potter's abode;*
There I'll cause you to hear My words;"
3 *Thus to the potter's house I strode.*

He wrought a work there on the wheels,
4 *But the vessel he made from clay*
Was marred in the potter's hand,
But he didn't throw it away,

Another vessel the potter made,
He molded from the clay again;
Formed from the very same clay,
A vessel that seemed good to him,

5 *The word of the Lord came again to me:*
6 *"Israel, can I not do with you,*

What the potter did to the clay in his hands,
Can I take clay and mold you anew?

7 *"When I speak concerning a nation,*
Or of a kingdom to pluck it up,
To pull it down and destroy it
Like pouring water out of a cup.

8 *"But if that nation, against I've spoken,*
Will turn back from its evil ways,
I'll relent of the evil thought to do them,
And I then will lengthen their days.

9 *"If again I speak of a nation,*
To plant and build it as I would,
10 *If it should then do evil in My sight,*
I'll turn from My plan to do good." ✝

Proverbs 22

1 *Instead of wealth seek loving favor.*
Instead of riches choose a good name.
2 *God made both the poor and the wealthy;*
In His eyes they are the same.

3 *A prudent man sees trouble coming.*
He prepares and takes a new direction.
But the simple pass on and suffer,
Because they failed to make correction.

4 *By humility and fear of the Lord*
One receives riches, honor and life.
5 *The wicked finds thorns and snares,*
But the righteous keeps his soul aright.

6 *Train up a child as he should go.*
Lead him down the straight, narrow path.

He will stay on that way when he's old,
And escape God's judgment and wrath.

7 *The rich rule over the poor,*
The borrower sells himself for gold.
8 *The sower of iniquity shall calamity reap,*
And the rod of his terror will grow cold.

9 *A man with a generous heart*
Will be blessed by God and his neighbor,
For he gives of his bread to the poor,
And he'll be repaid for his labor.

10 *Cast out the scorner while you can.*
Send contention away from your home.
Strife with the scorner will flee.
Quarrels and insults will be gone. ✝

Galatians 5:1-6, 14, 22-23

1 *It was for this freedom that*
Christ came and set us free.
Therefore, stand firm, don't take again
The yoke of slavery.

2 *Behold, I Paul, say this if you*
The circumcision receive,
Christ will be no benefit to you,
For you did not believe.

3 *To everyone who's circumcised*
A debtor is every man,
Bound by God to surely keep
The entire law's demand.

4 *You've been alienated from Christ*
By putting in His place,
Justification by the law
You've fallen away from grace.

5 *We by faith, through the Spirit wait*
For the hope of righteousness.
6 *Circumcision means nothing — it's*
Faith through love we confess.

14 *The entire law is fulfilled,*
In one single command,
Love your neighbor as you love yourself,
Is God's law for every man.

22 *But the fruit of the Spirit, you see,*
Is love and joy and peace,
Patience, goodness, faithfulness: Through
The Spirit, these don't cease.

23 *There's also gentleness, through*
The Spirit you've self-control.
Against such things there is no law,
The Spirit has made you whole. ✟

19 *When you speak to one another, speak
In psalms and spiritual songs,
Making melody to the Lord in your hearts
Will keep you from many wrongs.*

20 *Give thanks to God for all things, in
The name of Christ our Lord.*
21 *Be subject to one another as to Him,
Christ, the Living Word.*

22 *Wives be subject to husbands, the*
23 *Husband is head of the wife,*

*As Christ is the head of the church,
For which He gave His life.*

24 *He is the Savior of the body
The church is subject to Him.
So ought wives be subject to husbands,
Their love should never dim.*

25 *I say, husbands love your wives,
Just as Christ the church does love
He gave Himself up for it,
With a love that's from above.* ✝

Philippians 3:7-14

7 *But whatever was to my profit*
I count loss for Christ's sake.
8 *And more, I consider loss compared*
To the knowledge that I take

Of Jesus Christ my Lord and
His surpassing greatness.
For whose sake I lost all things
I think them trash, no less.

So that I may gain Jesus Christ
9 *And so in Him be found,*
Not in righteousness from the law
But where faith in Christ abounds.

And a righteousness which comes from God
When on Christ our faith we base,
10 *To know Christ and His life giving power*
And His sufferings embrace.

To become like Him in His death,
11 *That somehow I attain*
Life free from the power of sin —
Christ's resurrection gain.

12 *Not that this I've obtained, or that*
Perfection I've now acquired.
But pressing on to take hold of that
Which Christ's hold has never tired.

13 *I have yet to take hold of this,*
But by one thing I am led,
Forgetting that which lies behind
I am pressing on ahead.

14 *I press on toward the goal to win*
The prize for which God did call
Us up to heaven because of
What Jesus did for us all. ✞

Hebrews 13:1-3, 5-9

1 *At all times love your brothers;*
2 *Give hospitality*
To everyone, even strangers,
For angels they might be.

3 *Remember those in prison and*
Those given treatment shoddy
As though you suffer with them, since
You are in the same body.

5 *Do not let the love of money*
Be what controls your life,
But be content with what you have
And save yourself some strife.

God's said He'll not desert you, "My
Child I will not forsake."
6 *So we can say with confidence*
Of His blessings we'll partake.

We say the Lord's our helper, and
Afraid we'll never be,
"For if God is by my side what
Shall a man do to me?"

7 *Remember those who led you, who*
Spoke God's word unto you,
Consider now their way of life,
And such things likewise do.

8 *Jesus Christ is just the same*
Both yesterday and today,
Yes, He is the same forever,
And does not turn away.

9 *Don't be swayed by strange teachings; for*
It is good for the heart
To be strengthened by God's grace, but
With strange truths have no part. ✞

Ezekial 33:1-7, 9

1 *The word of the Lord came to me saying,*
2 *"Son of man, to My children speak:*
When I bring a sword upon the land,
Someone for a watchman you should seek.

3 *"When he sees his foes from afar,*
And his trumpet sounds the alarm;
4 *If one hears but heeds not the warning,*
He'll be captured and come to harm.

"His blood shall be upon his own head,
5 *For he did hear the trumpet sound,*
But the warning he did not heed,
No fault with the watchman can be found.

"Blessed is the one who heeds the warning
He is the one whom the Lord will save.

The Lord will deliver him from the enemy,
The Lord will deliver him from the grave.

6 *"But if the watchman sees his foes coming,*
And on the trumpet, he does not blow,
If the people should receive no warning
And to death and captivity they go,

"Their blood will be on the watchman's head.
7 *Son of man, a watchman I've made you;*
You shall hear the word from my mouth,
You shall tell the people what to do.

9 *"If you tell the wicked one to repent,*
And if he continues in his wicked way,
He shall die in his sin and iniquity,
But your soul will be delivered that day." ✝

Philippians 4:4-11

4 *Always rejoice in the Lord; again*
I say be of good cheer.
5 *Let your kindness be known to all,*
Tell them the Lord is near.

6 *Do not worry for anything,*
But in everything by prayer
Make your requests known unto God,
With Him your troubles share.

7 *Now God's peace which surpasses all*
That you can comprehend,
Will guard your hearts and minds in Christ,
Will keep you to the end.

8 *Finally brethren, whate'er is true,*
And honorable in God's sight,
Whatever is lovely and pure and
Whatever you know is right,

Whate'er is of good report, and
If it's worthy of praise,
Let your mind dwell on these things, as
To God your voices raise.

9 *Things you have learned and received,*
What you have heard and saw in me,
If you will practice all these things,
God's peace shall be with thee.

10 *I now rejoice in the Lord since*
You've shown your concern for me.
I know you were concerned before
But lacked opportunity.

11 *Not that I speak from want, for I*
Have learned to be content.
Regardless of circumstance, I
Accept what God has sent. ✝

1 Thessalonians 4:11 - 18

11 *You should make it your ambition*
To lead a quiet, peaceful life;
Attending to your own business
And thus avoid much strife.

Don't fear to work with your hands,
Just as we commanded you.
12 *Behave properly toward outsiders*
In everything you try to do.

13 *Now as to those who are asleep,*
In ignorance do not grope,
And do not grieve as do the rest
Who in Christ have no hope.

14 *If we believe Jesus died*
And that He arose again,
So God will raise those who sleep,
Those whom Christ freed from sin.

15 *We have this word from the Lord*
And this is what He said,
"Those who live until His coming
Shall not precede the dead."

16 *The Lord will descend from heaven*
And God's trumpet you will hear.
The archangel then will shout,
First those asleep will appear.

17 *Then we who are living still,*
The Lord also for us does care
We also shall be caught up
To meet the Lord in the air.

18 *Therefore, comfort one another,*
These words with others share.
Lighten each others' burdens
With tender loving care. ✞

1 Thessalonians 5:14-24

14 *Now we exhort all the brothers to*
Admonish the unruly in their sin,
Help the weak and fainthearted,
And to be patient with all men.

15 *Do not repay evil with evil*
Seek what is good for all men.
16 *Rejoice always and be glad,*
17 *Pray constantly within.*

18 *Give thanks always in everything;*
This is God's will for you.
19 *Do not quench the Spirit of God,*
Follow Him in all you do.

20 *Do not despise prophetic gifts.*
21 *Examine all things carefully;*
Hold fast to that which is good,
22 *Let no evil be found in thee.*

23 *May you be sanctified, I pray,*
May you be preserved complete;
To present your soul and body
At Jesus' blessed feet.

May you be blameless in that day,
When our Lord returns again.
24 *He will fulfill your calling;*
He will do it for you then. ✝

Hebrews 11:1-6, 8

1 *Now faith is the substance of*
The things we have not seen,
An assurance of things we hope for, a
Belief on which we lean.

2 *By it men gained divine approval,*
3 *And by faith we understand*
That the world was prepared by God, and
All things were made by His hand.

So what was seen was not made out
Of things which we can see,
But God made everything of nothing,
Including you and me.

4 *By faith Abel offered a sacrifice*
Which by God was accepted
God testified to his righteousness,
While Cain's gift was rejected.

God in accepting Abel's gift
Showed us what is desired;
And Abel, though he's dead, speaks,
To show what is required.

5 *By faith Enoch was taken up*
So death he should not see;
He was not found, for God took him
Saying, "Enoch has pleased Me."

6 *Without faith we can't please God, he*
Who seeks God must believe
That our God is the one true God
If rewards he's to receive.

8 *By faith Abraham obeyed the Lord*
When called unto a place
Which he'd receive as an inheritance,
According to God's grace. ✝

2 Timothy 1:6 - 12

6 *I'd have you start afresh and each*
Day, I'd have you renew
The gift of God which you received,
When I laid hands on you.

7 *God did not give us a timid spirit,*
But one of discipline, love and power.
8 *Therefore, don't be ashamed to speak*
Of our Lord at any hour.

And do not be ashamed of me
Though I am here in jail,
But join me in my sufferings.
God's power will prevail.

9 *God saves us and He calls us, not*
According to what we've done,
But in his long-held purpose, this
Through Jesus Christ, His Son.

10 *Through the appearing of Christ Jesus*
Our salvation's been revealed.
He abolished death, and brought life when
His world was not concealed.

11 *It was because of the gospel that*
I was appointed a preacher,
I also am an apostle, and
I have been called a teacher.

12 *For this reason I also suffer,*
But I am not ashamed,
For I know whom I've believed
And His child I became.

I am thoroughly convinced
He's more than capable, I say,
Of keeping that which to Him
Has been entrusted unto that day. ✝

Matthew 1:18-25

18 The birth of Jesus came like this:
Joseph thought he'd been deceived.
For although engaged to Mary
He found she had conceived.

19 A righteous man was Joseph,
To serve God he did aspire.
He balked to marry her, but to
Disgrace her had no desire.

20 An angel spoke in a dream.
This message he received:
"Joseph, take Mary as your wife,
For by the Spirit she's conceived.

21 "Jesus will be the Savior's name,
He'll save His people from their sin.
In Him God will live on earth
And touch the lives of men.

22 "All of this has come to pass,
Recall what God has willed:
23 'A virgin with child shall be'
This prophecy fulfilled.

"This virgin shall bring forth a son,
Immanuel shall be his name.
Immanuel means, 'God with us,'
You'll never be the same."

24 Joseph arose from his sleep,
And obeyed the Lord's command.
He took Mary as his wife,
Just as the Lord had planned.

25 He kept Mary as a virgin
Until her first born came.
He called this son, Jesus,
And blessed be His name. ✞

Luke 2:8-14

8 *Out in the fields nearby,*
Lived shepherds keeping sight
Of their flocks of sheep
While others slept that night.

9 *An angel of the Lord appeared to them*
And they were terrified,
As God's glory shone 'round about,
But then the angel cried:

10 *"Fear not, I bring good news for all,*
Great tidings I bring down.
11 *A Savior has been born to you*
In Bethlehem, David's town"

"He is Christ the Lord,
12 *And here's a sign for you:*
You'll find a baby, wrapped in cloth,
And lying in a manger, too."

13 *Suddenly a great choir arrived,*
A heavenly host were they.
Praising God with the angel,
The shepherds heard them say:

14 *"Glory to God in the highest*
Peace on earth, goodwill to men
On whom God rests His favor."
The angels all left then. ⚜

Mark 1:1-8

1 The beginning of the gospel
Of Jesus Christ, God's Son.
2 As foretold by the prophets
This good news is begun.

I send My messenger before You
Who will prepare Your way;
3 A voice cries in the wilderness
And this is what he'll say:

"Make ready for the Lord to come,
Yes, make His pathways straight."
Those who hear and believe His words
Will pass through heaven's gate.

4 John baptized in the wilderness.
Preaching that men should repent
To have their sins forgiven;
This is why John was sent.

5 The people of Judea came,
To hear John was their quest.
They were baptized in the Jordan river
After their sins they confessed.

6 John wore a cloak of camel's hair,
A leather belt around his waist.
His food was locusts and honey,
For them he had a taste.

7 He preached, "He who comes after me
Is mightier than I.
I am not fit to bow before Him,
Or His sandals to untie.

8 "I baptize you with water, but
He who's coming will
Baptize you and with
The Holy Spirit fill." ✞

Luke 2:41-51

41 *His parents went to the passover feast*
In Jerusalem each year;
42 *When He was twelve, He went along*
So the ritual He could hear.

43 *When the feast was over they started back,*
But Jesus stayed behind;
Mary and Joseph did not know
He had this thought in mind.

44 *They travelled all that day*
Thinking He was with friends;
They did not look for Him until
That day came to an end.

45 *And when they did not find Him, to*
Jerusalem they returned;
46 *They found Him after three days in*
The temple with the learned.

47 *Those who had heard Him were astonished*
At the things He understood,
They found Him very wise,
And His answers quite good.

48 *His parents were surprised, and said,*
"Son, what made You stay behind?
We have looked for You anxiously
Why did You trouble our minds?"

49 *Jesus then replied to them,*
"Why did you search for Me?
Did you not know in my Father's house
Is where I'd surely be?"

50 *They did not understand His statement,*
51 *But with Him did depart.*
Mary treasured all these words
And stored them in her heart. †

Matthew 5:1-10

1 *When Jesus saw the multitudes*
Moving like a mighty tide,
He went upon a mountain,
His disciples by His side.

2 *There he opened up his mouth*
And He began to teach,
3 *"Blessed are the poor in Spirit,*
Heaven's kingdom they will reach.

4 *"Blessed are they who mourn,*
They will find joy and mirth.
5 *Blessed are the meek and lowly,*
They will possess the earth.

6 *"Blessed are those who hunger*
And after righteousness do thirst,
Surely they will be satisfied
As Satan's bonds they burst.

7 *"Blessed are the merciful,*
Mercy they shall be given.
8 *Blessed are the pure in heart,*
They will see God in heaven.

9 *"Blessed are the peacemakers,*
They're my children, God will confess.
10 *Blessed are the persecuted*
For the sake of righteousness. ♱

Matthew 6:1,3-21, 24-34

1 *"Don't give your gifts just so*
You will be seen by men
Or no rewards will you receive
From your Father in heaven then.

3 *"But when you give an alm*
To one who is in need,
Let not your left hand know
Of your right hand's deed.

4 *"Do only this deed in secret, so*
Your Father in heaven will see.
He'll know what you have done,
And he will reward thee.

5 *"Don't loudly pray in public places*
To make others aware.
6 *Go to your room and close the door*
And meet your Father there.

7 *"Do not pray like the pagan*
Who prays in volumes ample.
8 *Your Father knows your needs,*
9 *So follow this example:*

"Our Father who art in heaven
Hallowed be thy name.
10 *Thy kingdom come, Thy will be done,*
On earth and heaven the same.

11 *"Give us this day our daily bread,*
12 *Forgive us as we forgive,*
13 *Prevent temptation so that we*
May free from evil live.

14 *"If you forgive others, then*
God will forgive you too.
15 *But if you don't forgive,*
God won't forgive you.

16 "And when you fast let not gloom
Accentuate your face.
Fasting to be seen by men
With God gets you no place.

17 "Instead, when fasting wash your face,
And look as you usually do.
18 Fast to be seen of your Father,
Who will render you your due.

19 "Store not your treasure on this earth
Where moth and rust destroy,
Where thieves break in and steal away
Those objects of your joy.

20 "Lay up your treasure in heaven, where
You have a better deal.
There moth and rust cannot destroy
Or thieves break in to steal.

21 "For where your treasure is, you'll find
There your heart will dwell.
So if your treasure in heaven lies,
God will protect it well.

24 "No one can serve two masters, this
Should come as no surprise.
One will be held in high regard,
The other he'll despise.

"You cannot God and mammon serve,
No this you cannot do.
25 And for this very reason I
Will say these words to you:

"Do not be anxious for your life,
Or what today you'll drink and eat.
Think not how you clothe your body.
Life is more than clothes and meat.

*"Life is much more than food,
And the body more than clothes.
26 Look at the birds of the air
Who neither reap nor sow.*

*"They never store away supplies,
Yet these the Father feeds.
Are you not worth more than they,
Won't God supply your needs?*

*27 "You may be fretful and distraught,
Be burdened down with care.
But you can't add a moment to
Your life, so why despair?*

*28 "The lilies do not toil or spin,
Yet grow in glorious ease.
29 Yet Solomon in all his wealth
Was not arrayed like these.*

*30 "If God clothes the grass so, that is
Today and burned tomorrow,
Will He not also care for you
Of little faith, in sorrow?*

*31 "Therefore don't be concerned about
What food you have to eat,
Nor worry about what you drink
Or if your clothes are neat.*

*32 "For all these things the Gentiles seek,
But your heavenly Father knows.
33 Seek ye first His kingdom, and
God will provide all those.*

*34 "Do not be anxious for tomorrow,
Leave it upon the shelf.
Each day has its own troubles, let
The future care for itself."* ✟

Matthew 7:7-14

7 "Ask and it shall be given you,
Seek it and you shall find.
Knock and it shall be opened by
Our Lord so good and kind.

8 "For everyone who asks, receives,
He who seeks shall find.
God will open many doors
To those of an inquiring mind.

9 "Would a father give a stone
If his son asked for a cake;
10 Or if he asked to have a fish,
Would give to him a snake?

11 "If you then who are evil
Know to give your children good,

How much the heavenly Father will
When asked; you know He would.

12 "If you would have kind treatment
This then you must do,
You must treat people as
You'd have them treat you.

13 "Enter by the narrow gate,
Hell's gate is broad and wide,
It leads to sure destruction and
There flows the teeming tide.

14 "The gate that leads to eternal life
Is quite narrow and small.,
And only a very few
Will find the gate at all." ✞

John 3:16-21

16 "For God so loved the world His only
Begotten Son He gave,
That whosoever believes in Him
His soul will surely save.

"He who believes will never perish,
But have eternal life.
17 God did not send His Son to judge
But save from sin and strife.

18 He who believes in Him is not judged,
But judgment has been done
For those who have no faith
In God's own holy Son.

19 "This is the judgment, I proclaim
Light has come unto men,
But men loved darkness more than light,
Because they're deep in sin.

20 "He who does evil hates the light
And from light turns away,
Lest all his deeds should be exposed
By light's bright shining ray.

21 "But he who's truthful seeks the light,
His deeds to be manifested;
As if wrought by a holy God,
For by God's light they're tested." ✝

John 4:6-14

6 *Jesus, tired from traveling,*
Sat down to rest and think.
7 *A Samaritan woman came to the well;*
Said Jesus, "Give Me drink."

8 *The disciples had gone to the city*
To buy some food to eat,
But Jesus had remained behind
And made the well his seat.

9 *The woman answered, said, "You're a Jew*
This I see quite clearly,
But Jews don't deal with Samaritans
So why ask this of me?"

10 *Jesus answered, "If you knew God's gift*
And He who asks of you
To give to Him a drink of water,
This is what you'd do.

"You'd say 'give me a drink,'
And living water I would give.
Your thirst would then be quenched and you
Would then begin to live."

11 *"Sir, you have neither rope nor bucket,*
The water's far from the top.
Where do you get this living water,
Does it from heaven drop?

12 *"Are you greater than our father, Jacob,*
Who gave to us this well?
He drew water for his family and cattle,
Their thirst He would dispel."

13 *Said Jesus, "Whoever drinks this water*
Will more water soon implore,
14 *But whoever drinks the water I give,*
He shall thirst no more." ✝

Luke 9:20-26

20 *And Jesus turned to His disciples,*
Said, "You who with Me trod,
Who do you say I am?" Peter answered,
"You are the Christ of God."

21 *He warned them all to tell no one,*
22 *"The Son of Man must suffer much*
   pain,
Be rejected by the elders, priests and
   scribes,
Killed and raised to life again.

23 *"If anyone would follow Me*
He must himself deny,
And daily gather up his cross,
And follow Me close by.

24 *"Whoever would save his life, it's lost,*
But if it's for My sake,
Then he will truly save it and
A disciple I will make.

25 *"What profit comes to any man*
If all the world he gain
And thereby lose and forfeit self?
All he will have is pain.

26 *"If you would be ashamed of Me*
And of my teaching, too,
Then when I come in glory I
Will be ashamed of you." ✝

Mark 9:2-10

2 *And after six days Jesus went*
Up into a mountain range,
There before Peter, James and John
His countenance did change.

3 *His garments became radiant,*
Dazzling white beyond compare;
4 *Elijah and Moses appeared and*
Talked with Jesus there.

5 *Peter spoke and said to Jesus,*
"Teacher, to be here's well,
Let us now make three shelters
In which you each may dwell."

6 *He knew not what he should say,*
For they were terrified.
7 *Then a cloud formed over them*
A mighty cloud quite wide.

A voice came from the cloud
Saying, "This is My beloved Son,
I would have you listen to Him
And hear what He has done.

"All of you can learn from Him,
From what He has to say."
8 *At once they looked around and saw*
The visitors had gone away.

9 *As they were coming down the mount*
To the disciples Jesus said,
"Do not tell of these things until
I've risen from the dead."

10 *They seized upon Christ's statement and*
Upon what they had seen,
"He says, 'I'll raise up from the dead,'
By this what does He mean?" ✝

Matthew 10:27-33, 39

27 "What I say to you in darkness,
Speak out so all can hear.
Proclaim upon the housetops
What is whispered in your ear.

28 "Do not fear those who kill the body
But not the soul as well;
Fear Him who kills both soul and body
And destroys both in hell.

29 "Do not two sparrows cost a penny?
And yet it will be found,
That it is known by your heavenly Father
When these fall to the ground.

30 "The hairs are numbered on your head,
31 Therefore, please have no fear.
You are worth much more than sparrows,
To God you are so dear.

32 "Those who confess me before men
I'll confess to my Father on high.
33 Those who deny me before men
Before my Father I'll deny.

39 "He who finds life within himself
Will see it slip away.
But if he gives his life for Me
He'll live again someday." ✝

Mark 10:13 - 27

13 *Some brought their children to Him*
So o'er them He would pray,
They were rebuked by the disciples
Who tried to send them away.

14 *Jesus looked on with displeasure,*
Said, "Bring them to Me, please,
For all of God's great kingdom does
Belong to such as these.

15 *"I say unless you, like a child*
Upon our God call,
You will not see His kingdom, no
You'll not get in at all."

16 *He took the children in His arms,*
And blessed all those He held.
He laid His hands upon their heads,
With them His blessing dwelled.

17 *As He was starting on a journey*
A man ran up to ask,
"Good Master, How gain I eternal life,
Just what should be my task?"

18 *Jesus said unto the man,*
"Why do you call Me good?
No one is good but God alone,
I'd have this understood.

19 *"Know all God's commandments well,*
Let no lie come from thee,
Don't murder, cheat, or steal,
Or commit adultery.

"You must give honor to your father,
And to your mother, too."
20 *The man said, "I've done this since youth,*
What else is there to do?"

116

21 *Jesus looked and loved him much,*
Said, "You need one thing more,
Sell your belongings, then give all
The money to the poor.

"Treasure in heaven you shall have
If you then follow Me."
22 *At this the young man turned away*
For he was rich in property.

23 *Jesus looking at His disciples,*
Said something they thought odd;
"It is hard for those who are rich
To find their way to God."

24 *At this the disciples were amazed*
So He said the words again,

"Children, how very hard it is
God's kingdom to enter in.

25 *"It's easier for a camel to*
Go through a needle's eye
Than for the rich to enter heaven,
No matter how they try."

26 *The disciples were astonished, for*
This principle seemed so odd,
But marvelous to comprehend
As are all the things of God.

They asked Him, "Who then can be saved?"
27 *Jesus said, "It's not of man,*
But with God all is possible
According to His plan." ✝

Luke 10:25-37

25 *Behold a lawyer came up to Him,*
To put Him to a test;
Said, "How can I find eternal life?
For this is now my quest."

26 *Jesus said, "What's written in the Law?*
What does it mean to you?
How do you interpret Holy writ?
You know God's Law is true."

27 *"That you shall love the Lord your God*
With all your soul and mind;
Love Him with all your heart and love
Your neighbor, is what I find."

28 *Jesus looked him in the eyes, and said,*
"The answer you did give,
If you will do all of these things
Then you will really live."

29 *To justify himself, the lawyer*
Asked so that all could hear,
"Tell me who is my neighbor, is
It someone far or near?"

30 *He answered him, "A man went from*
Jerusalem to Jericho;
It was a very dangerous journey,
But there he had to go.

"Along the way he met some robbers
Who beat him on the head;
They stripped the man of everything,
And left him there half dead.

31 *"By chance a certain priest came by,*
Passed on the other side;
He saw the man but journeyed on,
Pretending he had died.

32 "A Levite also came that way,
And saw him lying there;
He too passed on the other side,
He had no time to share.

33 "Then a Samaritan came along,
And saw him on the ground.
He was not worried by the fact
That thieves might be around.

34 "He came and touched him where he lay,
And when he heard his groans,
He poured oil and wine on his wounds;
Bound up his broken bones.

"He put the man on his own beast
And took him to an inn.
He watched o'er him throughout the night,
Until healing did begin.

35 "The next day he spoke to the
        inn-keeper, when
His bill he went to pay;
'Here is some money, take care of him,
If more, I will repay.'

36 "Which of these three was a neighbor to
The man whom to thieves fell?"
37 He replied, "The one who showed
        Him mercy."
Jesus said, "Go, and do as well." ✝

Matthew 16:15-21

15 *To the disciples He then said,*
"Now I would hear from you,
Who do you believe I am?
Now make your answer true."

16 *Simon Peter answered boldly,*
Gave answer clear and loud,
"You are the Christ, the Son of God,
With His might you're endowed."

17 *Jesus answered and said to him,*
"Simon, you are truly blessed,
For My Father has revealed to you
This truth which you've confessed.

18 *"And I tell you, you are Peter,*
On this rock My church I'll build,
Hell may beat against it, but
My church cannot be killed.

19 *"I'll give you the keys to the kingdom,*
According to God's will,
The things that you bind on earth
Will be bound in heaven still.

"The things which you loose on earth
Will be loosed in heaven too,
So use the keys I've given
For the work I have for you."

20 *Then Jesus strictly charged them,*
"You are to tell no one
That I am Jesus Christ, the Lord,
That I am God's Holy Son."

21 *Then He began to show His disciples*
By whom He would be killed,
How He would suffer many things;
That prophecy would be fulfilled. ✝

John 6:1-13

1 *After these things Jesus went away*
Across the Sea of Galilee.
2 *A great crowd followed Him,*
Signs from Him they would see.

3 *Up a mountain side, with His*
Disciples He took His seat,
4 *Passover at hand, Jesus said,*
5 *"Where buy we food to eat?"*

6 *He asked this to test Philip, for*
He knew what He would do;
7 *Said Philip, "Fifty dollars worth*
Is for each a bite or two."

8 *Andrew, Peter's brother, said,*
9 *"A lad has loaves and fish,*
Five of the one, two of the other
If that is what you wish.

"But the people are so many, that
Much more food must be found."
10 *Jesus said to His disciples, "Have*
Them sit upon the ground."

There present were five thousand men
Or somewhere there about;
11 *He took the food, then gave thanks and*
Began to pass it out.

12 *When all had eaten and had their fill,*
Jesus said to His disciples, "Rather,
Any food should be lost, go
And all the fragments gather."

13 *And so they gathered up the pieces*
From the leftovers of the bread;
They gathered up twelve baskets full,
Once everyone was fed. ✝

Luke 13:31-35

31 *Some Pharisees came up to Him,*
And they drew Him apart.
Said, "Herod wants to kill you, so
From here you'd best depart."

32 *"Go tell that old fox," Jesus said,*
"Today I've made some whole,
Tomorrow cast out demons, and
The third day reach My goal.

33 *"But I must go along My way,*
The mission must be fulfilled,
For outside of Jerusalem
No prophet should be killed.

34 *"Oh Jerusalem – Jerusalem,*
The prophets you have stoned,

You have killed those sent to you, for
You I would have atoned.

"As a hen gathers all her chicks around
And guards them with her wings,
But you would not come unto Me;
Your action judgment brings.

35 *"Behold! Your house is desolate*
And I say this to you,
You'll not see Me again until
You accept My word as true.

"And when that time has come, you will
Declare in one accord,
'Blessed is He that cometh
In the name of the Lord.' " ☦

John 10:10-17

10 *"I came that they might have life, and*
Have it abundantly;
11 *I am the shepherd of the sheep*
For them I die willingly.

12 *"He who's a hireling, not a shepherd,*
Not the owner of the sheep,
He runs when he sees the wolf,
The flock he will not keep.

"The wolf snatches some of them, and all
The rest he scatters wide.
13 *The hireling flees because he's hired*
And in them has no pride.

14 *"I am the good shepherd, as*
You all can clearly see;
I know all of My own sheep,
And My own sheep know Me.

15 *"Even as I know the Father,*
By the Father I am known.
I lay down My life for the sheep,
For them I will atone.

16 *"And other sheep I have as well*
Which are not of this fold;
I must bring all of them as well
Out of the rain and cold.

"They shall become one flock as soon
As My voice they all hear;
The sheep will have one shepherd, and
To Him they are all dear.

17 *"Therefore the Father loves Me; He's*
With Me as I'm with men,
Because I will lay down My life
To take it up again." ✝

Mark 13:3-11

3 *As from the Mount of Olives they looked,*
Four disciples asked Him privately,
4 *"Tell us when this thing will happen*
And just what the signs will be."

5 *Jesus cautioned, "Let none mislead you,*
6 *Many will come in My name,*
'I am He', each will say, and
To be Christ each will claim.

7 *"And when you hear of wars and such*
You are to have no fear,
For all of these things must take place
Before the end draws near.

8 *"Nation will rise against nation*
And kingdoms will go to war.
There also will be famines
And earthquakes will be in store.

"All of this will happen, then
And troubles playing part,
But these sorrows are just beginnings,
The sadness just a start.

9 *"Take heed, you will be delivered up;*
Before rulers and kings you see,
Be beaten in the synagogues,
All on account of me.

10 *"First to all the nations*
The gospel must be taught.
11 *Whenever you are arrested,*
And to trial brought,

"Do not worry beforehand
What you are to say.
Speak as led by the Holy Spirit
Who will guide you all the way." ✝

John 12:12 - 19

12 The next day, a great multitude
Had gathered in the street,
When they heard He was near, they all
Went out the Lord to meet.

13 They cut branches from palm trees,
And they began to sing,
"Blessed is He whom God has sent.
Is this not Israel's king?"

14 Jesus found a donkey, on
Which there was put a coat.
Then He climbed upon its back,
Just as the prophets wrote.

15 "Fear not daughter of Zion, see!
When your king will appear
Sitting upon a donkey's colt;
You'll know God's kingdom's near."

16 The disciples didn't understand at first;
But when Christ was glorified
They remembered what was written and
Things done before He died.

17 The crowd that was with Him when
He called Lazarus from the grave
And raised him from the dead,
All said, "Israel He could save."

18 The crowd went out to meet Him ere
He reached the city wall.
Because He had performed a sign
They said, "He's Lord of all."

19 The Pharisees said to one another,
"We are not doing any good,
The whole world's going after Him,
As we had feared it would." ✝

Matthew 22:31-40

31 "As for the resurrection, how
Is it that you've not read
What God has spoken unto you,
The things that He has said?

32 " 'I am the God of Abraham,
The God of Isaac, too.
I am the God of Jacob and
Another thing is true:

" 'God is God of the living, He
Is not God of the dead.'
And all of you would know this if
The Scriptures you had read."

33 The multitudes heard this, and at
His teachings were astonished,
34 But when the Pharisees heard He
Had the Sadducees admonished,

They got their heads together and
Devised another test.
35 They sent a lawyer to ask of Him,
36 "Which commandment is the best?"

37 "That you shall love the Lord your God
With all heart, soul, and mind;
38 Is the first and greatest commandment
Which in God's word we find.

39 "The second is like unto it,
And this I give to you:
To love your neighbor as yourself,
Yes, this you ought to do.

40 "Upon these two commandments hang
The Prophets and the Law."
The Pharisees made no reply
For they were filled with awe. ✝

Luke 22:13 - 20

13 They went and they found everything
Just as the Lord had said.
Then they prepared the feast so that
All of them could be fed.

14 And when time came, the apostles sat
Reclining at the table.
15 He said, "I long to share with you;
I'm so glad we are able.

"For soon I will be made to suffer,
16 I shall not eat again
Until it be fulfilled within
God's kingdom – only then."

17 He took a cup, gave thanks and said,
"This to you I declare,
Take the cup and pass it so
That all of you can share.

18 "For I now say this to you,
I will drink no more wine
Until God's kingdom comes to pass
And in glory shall I dine."

19 Then Jesus broke some of the bread
And He gave thanks for it.
He said, "Share this among yourselves,
And eat you all of it.

"This bread is my body, I say,
Which is given for thee;
In the future times when you do this,
You'll then remember Me."

20 In the same way He took the cup,
Gave thanks and passed it around.
He said, "This is My blood which is
Poured out upon the ground." ✝

John 14

1 *"Let not your heart be troubled;*
Believe in God, and in Me too.
2 *In My Father's house are many mansions,*
Which I go to prepare for you.

"If this weren't so, I would tell you
3 *And if I go to prepare,*
Be sure I'll come again, and I
Will come to take you there.

"I want you to be with Me forever,
This is why I say,
4 *You know where I am going, and*
You also know the way."

5 *Thomas spoke and said, "Lord, where*
You go we do not know;
Therefore, how can we know the way
Unless You tell us so?"

6 *Jesus softly said to Thomas,*
"I am the way, you see;
I also am the truth and life;
You come to God through Me.

7 *"If you had known Me, Thomas,*
You'd know My Father too;
From now on you know Him,
For now I live in you."

8 *Said Philip, "Lord, show us the Father*
And we'll be satisfied."
9 *Said Jesus, "Don't you know Me? I've*
Walked daily by your side.

"I've told you if you have seen Me,
You've seen the Father too,
For the Father dwells in Me, this should
Be apparent unto you.

10 *"Don't you believe I'm in the Father?*
In Me, God you can see.
The things I say and works I do, are
Because He lives in Me.

11 *"Believe Me that I'm in the Father*
And He in Me does dwell,
Or else believe on account of the works
Which do a message tell.

12 *"Truly I say to each of you,*
Don't doubt, believe in Me.
You'll do the works that I do, and
13 *Even greater works you'll see.*

"Because I'm going to My Father,
Prayer in My name is done.
I will do this so that the Father will
Be glorified in the Son.

14 *"Whatever you ask in My name,*
That is what I will do.
15 *If you love Me keep My commandments*
Is what I ask of you.

16 *"I will ask My Father, and another*
Comforter He will send
Who will be with you forever,
And He will be your Friend.

17 *"This Friend will be truth's Spirit, whom*
The world cannot receive
Because it does not know Him, for
In Him they'll not believe.

18 *"I will not leave you desolate,*
19 *Soon you'll see Me no more;*
I will again come to you but,
Not as I came before.

"Because I live, you shall live and
20 *In that day you will know*
That I am in the Father and
You are in Me, also.

21 *"The one who truly loves Me will*
Keep all of My commands,
And he will be loved by the Father,
My love He'll understand."

22 *Judas, not Iscariot, said to Him,*
"Lord, what has come about
That you'll disclose Yourself to us,
Yet leave the world in doubt?"

23 *Jesus answered and said unto him,*
"He who loves Me keeps My word;

Therefore My Father will love him,
That one He will undergird.

"For We will come unto him,
And there make Our abode.
We will ease his burdens,
And also share his load.

24 *"He who does not keep all My words*
Then Me he does not love;
The words you hear are not Mine, but
The Father's from above.

25 *"These things I have said to you while*
Abiding with you still,
26 *But the Holy Spirit whom the*
  Father sends
Will come and My place fill.

"He will teach all things, then you'll
Remember what I said,
The days we walked together, and
Along the paths were led.

27 "Peace I now leave with you;
My peace I give today;
Not as the world gives, do I give;
My peace goes not away.

"Let not your heart be troubled,
Nor let it ever fear.
28 You heard Me say I go away,
But that should bring you cheer.

"Yes, I truly will go away,
But come again I will.

I go to be with the Father, because
Greater than I, He is still.

29 "Now I have told you all these things
Before they come about,
So that when they do come to pass,
You'll believe and will not doubt.

30 "I will not speak much more with you,
The world's prince does appear,
And he has nothing in Me, but
This prince's time is here.

31 "I'd have the world know I love the
Father
And do what He demands.
Arise, let's go from here and be
Faithful to His commands." ✝

Mark 14:32 - 50

32 Coming to the garden of Gethsemane,
To those with Him He did say,
"Come sit here for a while with Me,
While I go to pray."

33 Peter, James and John were there.
34 He said, "My soul is grieved.
I feel I am at the point of death,
From My burden I'd be relieved.

35 "I want you to stay and watch
While to My Father I cry."
Then He prayed, "Lord, if possible
Please let this cup pass by."

36 He was praying, "Abba, Father,
Hearken to My plea,
Remove this cup, but I will drink
If it's Your will for Me."

37 He found the disciples sleeping, said,
"Simon are you asleep?
Could you not watch one hour,
Your eyes wide open keep?

38 "Keep watching and keep praying lest
Temptation find you out.
The spirit is very willing but
Your flesh is weak, no doubt."

39 He went away and prayed again,
The same words He did pray.
40 When He returned they were asleep
And knew not what to say.

41 He came to them a third time and
Said, "Are you still at rest?
Behold! the hour is now at hand
For Me to meet the test.

"Into the hands of sinners is
Betrayed the Son of Man,
42 Arise, let us be going, the
Betrayer is at hand."

43 Judas had a signal planned
So His enemies could work with ease,
44 He said, "'Whomever I shall kiss
It's Him you are to seize."

45 He went right up and kissed the Lord,
And said to Him, "Rabbi!"
46 Then the guards seized Jesus and
His hands began to tie.

47 One of those who stood nearby
With a sword then did appear,

He swung it at the high priest's slave
And he cut off his ear.

48 "Am I leading a rebellion?"
Jesus said unto the men.
"Is that why you come with clubs and swords
To capture Me then?

49 "I was with you in the temple courts
Teaching every day.
You did not arrest Me then, so
Fulfill what the Scriptures say."

50 When the disciples saw Him bound
They turned and ran away,
Fear gripped their hearts so suddenly,
They were afraid to stay. ✝

Matthew 27:20 - 26

20 The priests said to the multitudes,
"This we would have you do;
21 When Pilate says, 'Whom shall I
    release?'
Ask Barabbas be given you."

When Pilate asked, "Whom do you
    want?"
"Barabbas," they all cried.
22 "What then shall I with Jesus do?"
"Let Him be crucified."

23 "What has He done?" asked Pilate, but
The crowd just shouted more,
"Let Him be crucified!" they said;
They cried this o'er and o'er.

24 Pilate saw he could not prevail,
The crowd was in an evil mood.
He feared a riot would soon begin.
Afraid of the multitude,

He called for a bowl of water, and
In it he washed his hands.
"Of His blood I am innocent;
Fulfill your own demands."

25 "His blood be on us and our
    children,"
All the people cried.
26 Barabbas was released; Jesus
    scourged and delivered
To be crucified. ✝

John 19:16-22, 25, 30, 37-42

16 He sent Jesus to be crucified;
For us Christ bore this shame,
17 He bore His cross up the hill, Golgotha,
Called by its Hebrew name.

18 On that hill they crucified him,
It was a gruesome scene.
There was a man on either side
And Jesus hung between.

19 Pilate wrote an inscription there
Which bore the following news:
"This is Jesus Christ, the Nazarene,
Who is King of the Jews."

20 The inscription was written three ways—
In Latin, Greek and Hebrew.
As they were near the city it
Was read by many a Jew.

21 The chief priest said to Pilate, "The
Inscription o'er His head
Should not read, 'King of the Jews,' but,
'I am King of the Jews, He said'."

22 But Pilate said, "This I have written
And I'll not take it down;
It says He was a king, although
He wore no earthly crown."

The soldiers therefore did these things
25 While near the cross was seen
Jesus' Mother, Mary, wife of Cleophas,
And Mary Magdalene.

30 Then He said, "It is finished." And
Those standing by could hear it,
He closed His eyes and bowed His head,
And He gave up His spirit.

37 "They shall look on Him whom they
    pierced."
Elsewhere these words are read.
All prophecies were thus fulfilled.
He died just as they said.

38 Then Joseph of Arimathea, a secret
Disciple until that day,
Asked Pilate for the body, that
He might take it away.

Pilate gave Joseph permission, who then
Took the body from the site,
39 And Nicodemus came with him, who
First came to Christ at night.

Nicodemus brought both myrrh and aloes,
A hundred pound in weight.

40 They quickly wrapped the body in
    linen,
For it was getting late.

To wrap the body in linen and spices
Was a custom of the Jews,
41 And near the crucifixion spot
A garden was in view.

They took the body to this garden
Where a new tomb had been made.
This tomb, it was nearby,
No one in it had ever laid.

42 Because the preparation day
Was getting very near,
And because the tomb was close by, they
Buried Jesus' body here. ✞

Luke 24:1-10

1 *But on the first day of the week,*
Just at the break of day,
The women brought spices to the tomb.
2 *The stone was rolled away!*

3 *When they entered into the tomb*
His body they did not find.
4 *They wondered what had happened and*
Each was perplexed in her mind.

Two men in bright apparel came
And stood there by their side.
5 *The women bowed unto the ground*
For they were terrified.

The men approached the women and
Kindly to them said,
"Why do you seek the Living One
In tombs among the dead?

6 *"He is not here, He's risen;*
Remember how He spoke to you
While He was still in Galilee?
Now you know His words are true.

7 *"He said He'd be delivered into*
The hands of sinful men,
By them be crucified, but on
The third day rise again."

8 *They remembered the words He'd spoken*
9 *And they returned from the tomb.*
They told of what had happened to them
To all those in the room.

10 *Among them Mary Magdalene,*
Joanna, Mary, James' mother;
They told these things to the eleven,
Confirming one another. ✝

Luke 24:34-39, 41, 44-48

34 "The Lord is risen, and been seen
By Simon," the disciples said.
35 Then they told of their experience
And how He had broken bread.

36 As they spoke among themselves,
Suddenly Jesus they were seeing;
37 They were startled by His appearance,
They thought He was a spirit being.

38 He said, "'Why are you troubled? in
Your hearts why is there doubt?
39 Both see My hands and touch My feet,
There's evidence about.

"A spirit has not flesh and bones,
Or walks upon its feet."
41 Still they could not believe for joy
He said, "Have you any meat?

44 "All things that were written of Me,
Which the Law and Prophets said,
They all said I would suffer and
Then be risen from the dead."

45 Then He explained to them the Scriptures,
46 "Thus did God's Word say,
That Christ should suffer and rise from
The dead, for you on the third day.

47 "The Scriptures also plainly say
That repentance and remission of sin
Should be preached of Him to every nation
Beginning at Jerusalem.

48 "You are witnesses of these things;
You've seen them come to pass.
You know that God has spoken,
And Christ has come at last." ✝

Matthew 28:16 - 20

16 The disciples went to Galilee
Which He had designated,
17 When they saw Him they worshiped Him.
They were greatly elated.

They all fell down and worshiped Him,
But some were doubtful still.
18 Jesus came up and spoke to those
Who were gathered on the hill.

"All power has been given Me
In heaven and every nation.

19 Go therefore; make disciples,
Tell them of My salvation.

"Baptize them in the Father's name,
Of the Son and Spirit, too,
20 Teach them to observe all things
That I have commanded you.

"I will be with you always,
In all the things you do.
I'll provide the power to overcome
Until life on earth is through." ✝

1 John 4:15 - 21

15 *Whoever will confess that Jesus*
Is truly the Son of God,
Then God abides in him, and he,
Also abides in God.

16 *We know the love God has for us.*
We know and have believed.
God is love; he who abides in Him
God's love he has received.

17 *Love is perfected in us, that*
We may have confidence
That in the day of judgment, love
Will cover our offense.

Because as He is, so are we,
In this old world below.
18 *There is no fear in love, for love*
Casts out fear, you should know.

For fear's involved with punishment.
The one who is afraid
Has not, in His love, been perfected
In the true mold God made.

19 *We love because He first loved us.*
20 *If one says, "I love God,"*
But then his brother hates, he has
Not God's approving nod.

For if he does not love his brother,
Whom he has often seen,
How can he therefore love our God
Who to him is still unseen?

21 *And this command we have from Him,*
Not a command that's new,
But that the one who would love God
Should love his brother, too. ✝

Titus 3:1-8

1 *Have them be subject to rulers and*
Those in authority.
To be ready to do good deeds
And this obediently.

2 *Remind them to malign no one,*
Not quarrel, be gentle too,
With consideration for all men
In all you say and do.

3 *We also once were foolish, both*
Defiant and deceived,
Enslaved to lust and pleasure. In
Christ we had not believed.

We spent our lives in malice, full
Of envy, full of strife,
Hateful, hating one another.
That was our way of life.

4 *When the kindness of our Savior and*
His love for man appeared,
5 *We weren't saved by our deeds, but by*
His mercy we were cleared.

By the washing of rebirth and
New by the Holy Spirit,
6 *Whom He poured out on us richly,*
Though not due to our merit,

7 *But being justified by His grace*
That we would be His heir,
This in the hope of eternal life
Which with our Lord we'll share.

8 *This thing I know is true. About*
These things I'd have you speak,
So that those who believe in God will
Only righteous deeds seek. ✝

1 John 5:1 - 5, 11 - 14

1 *If you believe Jesus is the Christ,*
Born of God's holy stem,
Whoever loves the Father loves
The child born of Him.

2 *Hence, we know we love God's children,*
When we love God, and serve.
3 *For this is the love of God, that His*
Commandments we observe.

His commands, they are not burdensome,
A light yoke upon the neck,
4 *For whatever is born of God*
Does hold the world in check.

Faith in Christ brings victory,
The world it will overcome.
5 *The overcomer is the one*
Who believes Christ is God's Son.

11 *This is the testimony, that*
God gave us eternal life,
And this life is in His Son Who
Will end our earthly strife.

12 *He who has the Son has life,*
He who has not is dead.
Only with Christ can we live forever,
Despite what the world has said.

13 *I've written to you who believe*
In the name of God's Son
So you will know eternal life
Through Christ is already won.

14 *This is our confidence in Him,*
If we ask in His will,
He hears our earnest pleas and our
Requests He will fulfill. ✝

2 Peter 3:8-14

8 *Don't let this fact escape your notice,*
Heed what the Lord does say,
One day is as a thousand years, and
A thousand years one day.

9 *The Lord's not slow about His promise*
The way some think Him slow,
But He's patient toward you, wanting
All, the good news to know.

He doesn't want any to perish,
But He wants all to repent,
10 *The day of the Lord comes as a thief,*
Be ready for this event.

The heavens will all pass away
The elements will be destroyed,
The earth will be burned up, along
With those works we've all enjoyed.

11 *Since all will be destroyed, what sort*
Of people should you be?
In holy acts and godliness,
What God would have you be.

12 *Looking for and speeding the coming day*
When God on earth we'll meet,
The heavens will be burned up and
Elements will melt with heat.

13 *But by His promise, we look for*
A new heaven and earth,
In which all righteousness abounds
And all is joy and mirth.

14 *Beloved since you await these things*
Be strong in all you do
To be found spotless and blameless
When He returns for you. ✝

Revelation 1:1 - 8, 13 - 16

1 *The revelation of Jesus Christ*
Which God gave Him to show
To His bond servants
Things they ought to know.

Things which soon will come to pass;
For the time will soon be gone.
He sent this message by His angel
To His bond servant John.

2 *Who bore witness to God's word*
And to Christ's testimony.
Even everything he saw
He reported to you and me.

3 *Blessed is he who reads these words*
And hears the prophecy without doubt,
And heeds the things written in it
For they will soon come about.

4 *John to the seven churches*
That are found in Asia's land.
Grace to you and peace from Him
Upon whose authority I stand.

He is the One who always was,
And is the One who's coming too,
And from the seven Spirits before His throne
I write these words for you.

5 *From Christ the faithful witness*
The first born of the dead,
Ruler of the kings of earth,
Come, listen to what He's said.

He is the One who loves us,
By His blood He released us from sin,
6 *He has made us to be kings and*
Priests, who will rule with Him.

We will stand before His God and Father.
To Him be glory and dominion,
It should be given to Him,
This is my true opinion.

7 Behold! He is coming,
He is coming in a cloud,
And every eye will see Him,
Every knee will be bowed,

Even those who pierced Him.
When on earth He comes again
All tribes will mourn o'er Him,
Even so Lord, I say "Amen."

8 "I am the Alpha and Omega,
I am the Beginning and the End;
Who was and is and is to come,"
Says the Lord God our creator, friend.

13 In the middle of the lampstands
Was one like the Son of Man
Clothed in a robe reaching to His feet,
Across His breast a gold girdle ran.

14 His head and hair were white like wool,
Or perhaps you'd say, white like snow.
His eyes were like a flame of fire
As He gazed on me below.

15 His feet were like burnished bronze,
Which a furnace caused to glow,
His voice, the sound of many waters,
You could hear where e'er you'd go.

16 In His right hand were seven stars,
From His mouth came a two-edged sword;
His face was like the sun in strength,
This is how I saw the Lord. ✝

Revelation 21:1 - 6

1 *I saw a new heaven and a new earth*
For the first had passed away,
And there is no longer any sea
To hold the saints at bay.

2 *And I saw the holy city,*
It was a new Jerusalem
Coming from God out of heaven,
Like a bright and shining gem.

The new city was made ready as a bride,
It was so beautiful and fair,
Adorned as for her husband
Whom she will meet in the air.

3 *I heard a voice from the throne,*
Saying, "Behold, God's tabernacle
Is now to be found with men
And with them He shall dwell.

"They shall be His people,
And among them He will be,
He is the great and mighty God,
As all the universe can see.

4 *"He shall wipe tears from their eyes,*
There will be no more death or pain;
The first things have passed away
And will not come back again."

5 *And the one who sits on the throne*
Said, "Behold I make all things new."
And He said, "Write this down,
For it is faithful and also true."

6 *And He said unto me,*
"It is done. My friend,
I am the Alpha and the Omega,
The Beginning and the End." ✝

Revelation 22:16 - 21

16 "I, Jesus, have sent My angel to
Testify this unto you.
The churches need to know what's coming,
And know My words are true.

"I am the Root, Offspring of David,
The Bright and Morning Star,
And all those who believe in Me
From heaven I'll not bar.

17 The Spirit and the Bride say, 'Come.' "
The one who hears says, 'Come.'
These words go out to all believers
No matter where they're from.

"If anyone is thirsty, then
Let him come to the brink

Of the spring of living water,
Without cost let him drink.

18 "I warn those who hear what's written
In this book of prophecy,
If someone adds to them, God adds
This book's plagues unto thee.

19 "If someone takes away from these
Words, God shall take his part
From the tree of life and the holy city,
which this book did impart.

20 The Testifier's coming quickly."
Come, Lord Jesus. Come again.
21 The grace of the Lord be with the saints.
Again, I say, Amen. ✝

Index

S

T

Ripples of Light

Scriptural Reflections in Rhyme

Here's a wonderful gift idea. Send in this coupon to order *Ripples of Light* and we'll include a free gift envelope for each book you order.

To order, send $4.95 for each book plus $2 shipping & handling for the first book, .50 each additional copy.

Please send _____ copies of *Ripples of Light*.

☐ Payment enclosed (check or money order) Bill my ☐ VISA ☐ MasterCard

☐☐☐☐-☐☐☐☐-☐☐☐☐-☐☐☐☐ ☐☐/☐☐ _____
Card Number   Exp. date   Cardholder Signature

Send books to: _____

Address_____

City _____State _____Zip _____

Mail to: HANNIBAL BOOKS, 921 Center St., Hannibal, MO 63401.
For quantity discounts call 800-747-0738. Satisfaction guaranteed or full refund.

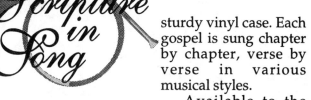

There's a sweet, sweet sound in these tapes.

It's music to the ears when you experience *The Rhyming Gospels* set to music. Each gospel is contained in a set of 3-4 cassette tapes which are packaged together in a sturdy vinyl case. Each gospel is sung chapter by chapter, verse by verse in various musical styles.

Available to the public for the first time, this is a delightful new way to enjoy God's Word.

The gospels are available individually for \$24.95, or as a 4 volume set for \$89.95.

Send ☐ copies of Matthew, ☐ copies of Mark, ☐ copies of Luke, ☐ copies of John.

Send ☐ 4-volume set

Send tapes to: _____

Address_____

City _____State _____Zip _____

Mail with check or money order to: LIVESHOP PUBLISHING, 3807-L Dickerson Road, Nashville, TN 37207. Phone 615-865-0553. Satisfaction guaranteed or full refund.